# Erotic Slavehood

## The Miss Abernathy Omnibus

Christina Abernathy

Published in the United States by Greenery Press, 4200 Park Blvd. pmb 240, Oakland, CA 94602, www.greenerypress. com.

ISBN 1-890159-71-9.

# Contents

# Foreword
## by Laura Antoniou

I'm the last person who should introduce this book.

No, really. After all, it's all my fault people have such inaccurate images of what it means to serve and to be served. OK; perhaps not all my fault, but certainly I belong to the class of people most responsible for the shocking cognitive dissonance surrounding service in an SM context. We fiction writers have (maliciously, perhaps) planted the mutually conflicting positions 1) Service is an inborn desire, held by many and 2) Service is a serious vocation requiring great effort and achieved by few. To add even more spice to this stew, we also suggest that the desire to be served both inspires the offering of service all by itself and that it requires incredible self-discipline, education and great effort, a combination again achieved by few.

I'd offer a mea culpa except that's not my thing. Anyone who actually knows Laura, and not "the author of the Marketplace books," knows that I loathe the very idea of someone basing their real life activities on fiction. Theme parks are great fun and I love 'em. But I don't live in one, despite what people think of New York.

However, despite my fiction-writing proclivities, I also harbor a deep and personal identification with the world of genuine service-oriented submission – a philosophy which I fully admit to weaving into my make-believe worlds. I do believe there are those for whom service is a sort of calling; a way in which they find sexual, emotional or other fulfillment. I also believe there are those for whom being served in such a way – voluntarily and with a sense of obligation and responsibility – is a profoundly satisfying and exciting proposition. And I believe that the matching of one to the other is the very best reason for our entire community to exist.

However, because this is real life and not fiction, the mere connection is not nearly enough. If it were, no one would read fiction, they'd be too busy enjoying their real lives. (It's true, mine is a profession which relies on people being dissatisfied.) Instead, there are formidable stumbling blocks and detours on the way to happy and fulfilling service.

To begin with there are those who fantasize. They believe they have this urge to serve, at least when they are alone with their eyes closed. For a million reasons, however, they will not actually move from fantasy. They have partners, spouses, family responsibilities, professions, goals, physical and emotional ailments, fears and worries, all of which stand in their way of even considering how to actually do anything about it.

Then there are the planners. They fully intend to find someone they can serve, and to do useful things in an SM context. They want to experience the reality in one way or another, but their limitations are slightly more subtle than the fantasists. They will enter service one day – after they learn French. When the kids are grown. When the divorce is final. When they find the perfect person – of course. Having identified what they believe to be the power which holds them back, they need only finish that project, reach that goal, and then they will be ready!

And then there are those who actually try it.

This volume belongs to them.

Here you will find no spicy tales of bondage and whipping, dainty and impractical costumes, sweeping romances or brutal, edgy violence. Those who are ready to put their bodies and minds in motion know where to find the smut when they want it. (Did I mention I write smut?) What they lacked were realistic guides, inspirational and practical, with a judicious eye for the rewards and drawbacks of service and a healthy sense of humor.

That is, until Miss Abernathy.

After all, there are guides to almost anything someone can do for someone else. Down at the local bookstore, you can find shelves and shelves of manuals on cleaning, cooking, household management, accounting, catering, computer programming, entertaining and, of course, sex. Childcare? Animal husbandry? Shopping? No problem, you can find websites dedicated to the topics. Hair styling, leather care, electrical wiring, running a garage sale, making travel arrangements, finding directions to Bayonne? It's out there. But if you were looking for something specifically aimed at those for who wanted to offer personal service in our multi-named lifestyles, pickings were slim. Ironing the sheets because you like the feel is the province of Martha™. Ironing them because Mistress will be pleased and you feel rewarded – that was an inspirational angle not sufficiently acknowledged anywhere.

Except for Miss Abernathy.

I was always very happy to tell people which books I had on my shelves, whether I used them for research or practical purposes. But there's a big difference between, say *Home Comforts,* my answer to all things domestic, and the wit and wisdom of Miss Abernathy. Abernathy is talking to me. And, if you are beyond fantasy and planning, she is talking to you. I would advise listening. From the first time I read these books, I thought, "This is someone who knows; this is the real goods." And then I'd stop and laugh – because sometimes what we do is pretty darn funny, and it takes a skilled writer to be able to communicate that with grace. People have asked me when I will write a non-fiction book explaining how to provide service – my answer has been, for years, there already is one. In an earlier review, I wrote of Miss Abernathy, "Chris Parker would approve."

I fully support that statement and add simply that Laura Antoniou does, too. I could only wish for more of her sage advice and sly wit on my shelves.

– Laura Antoniou, April 2007

# Editor's Notes

Miss Abernathy's gain is the BDSM scene's loss. She is living the happy ending to her own story: retired from the scene and living with the slave of her dreams in a small Northeastern town. She is no longer interested in writing about dominance and submission, preferring instead to enjoy their fruits.

In updating her words for a new generation of masters, mistresses and slaves, I find myself struck anew by how adroitly she manages a nearly impossible task: honoring the potent erotic drives and desires that drive people to own and be owned, while acknowledging the inherent challenges in making such dreams a reality.

Nothing about either the desires or the challenges has changed significantly in the decade since the original publication of *Miss Abernathy's Concise Slave Training Manual* and, later, *Training With Miss Abernathy: A Workbook for Erotic Slaves and Their Owners*. Thus, I have left her words intact except in those cases where external changes have created new possibilities (for example, personal ads these days are found more often in specialized websites than in print magazines).

However, one change could not have been anticipated even by the savvy Miss A: countless hours have been spent in angels-on-the-head-of-a-pin arguments about the difference between a "submissive" and a "slave," a "dominant" and a "master" or "mistress."

Miss Abernathy's original text uses the terms "submissive" and "dominant" to describe those who desire the relationship she describes, and "slave" and "master" or "mistress" to describe those who have attained it. Given that the semantic fistfights are now in their twenty-seventh round with no winner yet declared, I have left her terminology intact. The principles she describes are sound whether you call yourself a submissive, a slave or an artichoke. Feel free to substitute the noun of your choice for the ones she has used.

As in all general-interest Greenery Press books, every effort has been made to be gender-inclusive. You will see submissives, dominants, owners and slaves of all genders and orientations within these pages.

The Resource Guide in the back pages has been updated to the best of my ability. However, I am dismayed (and feeling rather elderly) as I note how many of the resources Miss Abernathy cited in her original texts are no longer extant. I have updated them as thoroughly as possible, but undoubtedly the lifetime of this new volume will see many of these new resources succumbing to the realities of all leather businesses and organizations: financial difficulties, changing relationships, shifts in scene demographics, life transitions and more. If the entity that you're trying to reach is no longer available, any good web search engine should turn up others of its kind.

Likewise, many of the texts in Miss Abernathy's Bibliography have gone the way of all (well, most) books: they are out of print. Most can be obtained through a good used-book search engine like the one at www.abebooks.com. I have also added books published in the last decade that I believe to be relevant to her teaching.

Welcome to Miss Abernathy's world, and may it help you discover the lifestyle you desire.

– Janet W. Hardy, April 2007

# Miss Abernathy's Concise Slave Training Manual

# Prelude in D

She is coming to my home tonight for the first time. We have met before, but only in public, at cafés and art galleries. She always arrives before me, not wishing to be late, but she waits patiently for me to arrive. She leaves me the most comfortable seat.

But tonight, she is coming to me, to my home, to serve me. I have given her clear instructions: she must arrive on the dot of eight. Under her conservative business suit, she will wear white stockings and garters; she will carry high-heeled white pumps in her bag. She will wear no jewelry for tonight; I will adorn her.

When I hear the cautious knock at the door, I do not rise. I call to her; she enters, closes the door behind her. Not once does she turn her back on me. I am watching.

I gesture for her to approach me, and she does, on her hands and knees, crawling gracefully across the floor. She stops within hand's reach and folds her body neatly, legs tucked under her and palms upturned on her thighs. Her head is bent, and her long hair falls forward, away from the nape of her neck: her beautiful, naked neck. I touch her and she shivers. I lift her chin with my finger and trace her collarbone with my gloved hand.

"Why are you here?"

"To serve you, Mistress." Her voice is soft and light and only trembles a little.

"You agree to obey me and to let my will be yours for this evening, as we have discussed?"

"Yes, Mistress. I would be honored, Mistress."

A lovely touch, that last. And I know I have chosen well this time.

I reach for the collar, the smooth metal links that will appear so heavy on her slender neck. She wants to follow my hand with her eyes, but I have not given her permission to, so she waits as I have left her.

"Kneel up!"

She raises herself up so that I can reach her more easily. I push her hair back over her shoulders and then gesture for her to hold it up. I can see the pulse in her lovely throat as the metal chain encircles it like a hand.

"As long as you wear this collar, you are mine to command. And until I remove it from your neck, I will consider you my responsibility, my possession, my slave."

She shudders almost imperceptibly.

Tonight she has come to me. And she is mine.

# Introduction

---

**In which we strive to make a good beginning by defining our terms and setting out our plans.**

---

Gentle Reader...

Perhaps you picked up this book out of mere curiosity, a slender volume like many others on a bookstore shelf. Or perhaps the title caught your eye, the words "slave training" flashing out like a beacon. Perhaps you have fantasized about dominance and submission for years but thought that masters and slaves only met in badly written paperbacks. Perhaps you are a dominant in search of a slave. Perhaps you are a submissive who yearns to serve but does not know where to begin. Perhaps you are a more experienced person in search of a detailed discussion of slave training, as distinct from other types of dominant/submissive play.

Consider this a primer, a simple and concise manual of consensual dominance and submission. It is not a pornographic novel, nor is it a directory of professional dominas. It does provide some background information, a reading list, a history lesson or two, and, at its heart, a simple program for training erotic slaves.

# What is "BDSM"?

Before we begin, it is vital that we define some of the specialized vocabulary used when discussing slaves and their training.

BDSM is a convenient shorthand for several overlapping terms: B/D refers to "bondage and discipline"; D/S to "dominance and submission"; and S/M to "sadism and masochism." While different people mean different things by these terms, for the purpose of this book, we shall define them as follows: bondage and discipline, as the name implies, refers to a wide range of activities including physical restraint and "punishment." It sometimes involves fantasy role-play. Sadomasochism covers all of the physical techniques that produce intense sensation, and the enjoyment of same. Dominance and submission refers to a consensual arrangement in which one partner takes the lead and the other follows that lead. It generally involves some form of role-play, and may or may not make use of bondage, discipline, or S/M techniques like whipping. There are many excellent introductions to BDSM available; if you are unfamiliar with the basics, check the Bibliography at the end of this book.

# What BDSM is not

Critics of dominant/submissive lifestyles like to remind us of the atrocities committed against human beings under the name of "slavery," from the ancient Greeks on down to the United States in the 19th century. Because of its historical resonance, many people find the very term "slave" offensive.

The distinction between BDSM and barbarism can be summed up in one word: consent. To avoid confusion, I reserve the term "slavery" for the sort of violence visited on African-Americans, among others, in the seventeenth, eighteenth, and nineteenth centuries. When speaking of consensual erotic submission, I use the term "slavehood." I prefer the word "slavehood," because it expresses a personal vocation rather than a social institution.

Some people enjoy fantasy role-play in which their chosen roles parallel historical types: plantation owner and black slave, or Greek prince and captive barbarian warrior. Again, the key word here is "chosen." We are talking about consenting adults making rational, informed decisions about their own lives. For submissives who fantasize about being owned or possessed, these roles may provide the ultimate satisfaction. Real slavery is illegal, as is pandering; erotic role-play, despite the efforts of the religious right, is not.

Just as BDSM is not about literally owning human beings, it is also not equivalent with abuse, sexual or otherwise. If you have any questions regarding this assertion, please reread the paragraph on consent above. If you still have questions about this topic, read one or more of the introductory books listed in the resource directory before proceeding.

# How is D/S different?

What distinguishes dominance and submission from other types of BDSM? If you accept the premise that the brain is the largest human sex organ, then BDSM is truly a mind-game. In the case of dominant/submissive play, this is doubly true. For unlike S/M or B/D, D/S is essentially a question of mind over matter. No elaborate dungeons or sex-toy collections are necessary. Instead, both the dominant and the submissive bring their intelligence and will into play. Submission depends on the individual's ability to align his will with that of the dominant and to use his intelligence to fulfill her wishes gracefully and efficiently. The dominant, for her part, must be ready and able to direct the submissive's will with her own.

Dominant/submissive relationships are role-based. A role-based relationship is, as the term suggests, one in which the dynamic between the partners is dictated by their chosen roles. The roles constitute the essence of their union, insofar as those roles are chosen to express the qualities in each that bind them, one to the other. Examples of role-based D/S relationships are Mistress-slave, Headmaster-schoolboy, or Trainer-puppy. A role-based relationship is by nature ongoing, but it can encompass everything from the occasional weekend scene to a full-time contract.

This program focuses on the practical training of personal slaves. It presupposes that not only does the dominant enjoy the simple act of commanding obedience, but he also has specific needs. Floors to be swept. Meals to be prepared. Boots to be polished, or worshipped, or both. In other words, the type of D/S interactions described here have service at their heart.

Now that we have our definitions in place, let us turn to the matter at hand.

# Part One: The Training Program

---

## In which we examine the specifics of training an erotic slave.

---

While the actual training of a slave encompasses the total person, the *sine qua non* of a service-oriented submissive is the correct attitude. Different roles may dictate different training techniques, but all slaves – and dominants, too, for that matter – should cultivate an attitude of mindfulness.

For our purposes, mindfulness may be defined as an overarching awareness of one's person, surroundings, and circumstances. It is a gentle attention, focused but not forced. Many spiritual traditions recommend sitting, chanting, or other forms of meditation to awaken a mindful state. For the slave, it is dharma yoga, the pursuit of one's true vocation, that is the path to mindfulness. A slave's mindfulness should encompass her physical body, her mental awareness, her emotional state and, insofar as it is possible, the physical, mental, and emotional state of the dominant and any other person in the environment.

This is not to say that a slave must be clairvoyant or an empath; she must first cultivate self-awareness, and under tutelage, awareness of the dominant's needs and wishes. Experienced slaves do often develop a sort of sixth sense, the ability to anticipate the dominant's needs before he verbalizes them.

# The interview

How can a dominant determine the best sort of training for a would-be slave? Before being accepted for formal training, a submissive should be interviewed by the prospective owner. The interview is an opportunity for both parties to learn something about the other's expectations and needs, to ask questions, express concerns, and generally familiarize themselves with the workings of the other's mind. The submissive may have questions about the dominant's style of training and interests, and the prospective owner should take care to answer these as honestly and directly as possible, to avoid any misunderstandings or unwitting deceptions. The dominant should be aware that submissives are often hesitant to ask direct questions and often must be prompted to do so. If the dominant maintains an attentive but relaxed demeanor, he will help put the submissive at ease.

To determine a submissive's suitability for training, it is vital that the dominant have extensive information about the person. Such information includes, but is hardly limited to, the following:

- the slave's full legal name and address
- all existing medical conditions and a general medical history
- any required medications and their whereabouts (it is wise to lay in a supply of them at the dominant's home or wherever the training will take place)
- emergency contacts and limitations to same, such as doctors, family members or friends, and therapists, and how much or how little personal information may be revealed to them in the event of an emergency

- any psychological limitations to play, such as abuse or incest history

Other information may include fantasies, sexual history, attitudes about submission, desires and preferences, and any interesting details a dominant may uncover during the interview. It is appropriate to take notes and keep a written record of the proceedings, but the dominant should encourage the submissive to speak freely, as one may learn as much if not more about a person by listening as by watching. Be alert for physical and verbal signs of ambivalence or hesitation, fear, or apprehension – pausing, blushing, hedging, or squirming. These are not necessarily indications that the submissive is unsuited for service, but they provide excellent opportunities for the dominant to explore areas that the submissive is not consciously aware of or is ashamed of. It is remarkable how little attention people pay to their own speech, particularly when they are excited and nervous. By listening carefully to a submissive during the interview, the dominant can later create the illusion of being a mindreader or of having "secret" information about the slave.

A series of interviews should be conducted before any arrangement is made or contract signed, and at regular intervals thereafter. For an ongoing contract, once a month is reasonable. Both parties should be given ample opportunity to gain the necessary information to make an informed decision about the training. The results of these interviews should be kept in a file in a locked box, along with a copy of the contract and any personal documents relating to the slave. A contract should include a clause specifying whether this file will be turned over to the submissive in the event that the relationship ends, whether the dominant may keep a copy of some or all of the information, and to what extent such information may be shared with others (when negotiating to bring another dominant into the scene, for example).

It is appropriate for the dominant to request from experienced submissives a sort of résumé of service previously provided or at least a list of references. Likewise, submissives should be provided upon request with the names of those who can vouch for the dominant's credibility.

The dominant may also require other documentation from the submissive, such as letters of petition, fictional narratives of the submissive's fantasies, journal entries (see below), or verification of the submissive's qualifications for specific forms of service, such as a valid driver's license and clean driving record from a prospective chauffeur.

It should be understood that such preliminary interviews, while expressive of a mutual interest in training, do not imply any obligation on the part of the dominant to take on the submissive, nor on the part of the submissive to accept any training program offered.

# The slave journal

Slaves-in-training should be encouraged to keep a written record of their thoughts, fantasies, and experiences. The journal is usually the property of the submissive but is meant to be read by the dominant. Thus, the dominant may require that the slave address the journal directly to her and that special written forms be followed.

For example, it is common for slaves to use the lower case when referring to themselves and to capitalize all references to the dominant: "Mistress, i am writing this journal as You requested. i hope it meets with Your approval." Or, they may be required to omit the first person pronoun altogether: "this slave is writing a journal as You requested." Some dominants find the use of the possessive in reference to themselves highly offensive, as the Mistress does not belong to the slave. They feel it is more appropriate for a slave to speak of "the Mistress" than of "my Mistress." Holding to this pattern can result in some interesting linguistic difficulties, but greatly encourages mindfulness. It is to be used at the dominant's discretion. Entries should be made in the journal on a regular basis (anywhere from once a day to once a week has proved useful). The dominant may wish to respond, verbally or in written form, to the entries.

# Other written training assignments

In addition to the slave journal, the dominant may assign essays on specific topics of interest, such as the history of erotic servitude or tea service. Book reports on BDSM classics have proved edifyng (see Bibliography for a selective reading list). The dominant may uncover a hidden talent for verbal expression – a useful and attractive attribute in a slave – that he may want to further encourage. At very least, he will have better insight into the submissive's thoughts and frame of mind.

# Physical preparation

Slaves should be encouraged to care for their bodies so that they will be better able to serve the dominant and so that such service will be more pleasing. Many dominants require that their slaves shave off their body hair, either just the pubic hair, or all of it. The feeling of nakedness and vulnerability this simple change can produce should not be underestimated. Men often find shaving their body hair humiliating, particularly if they associate shaving with women or femininity. Reactions like these provide an excellent opportunity to uncover unexamined prejudices that the slave may carry. Prejudices are an unnecessary burden that is best laid aside as quickly as possible. The slave will need his strength for other, more pressing matters.

The dominant may also require that the slave give herself a cleansing enema or douche as a preparation for service, or the dominant may wish to administer the enema herself. In either case, make sure that the enema is admistered properly, with no additives, warm but not hot water, and low water pressure. Commercial preparations can be used in a pinch, but water is most effective and is unlikely to cause unpleasant reactions. (Some individuals add a small amount of salt to help prevent undue fluid absorption.) Soaps and any form of alcohol should be avoided. The nozzle should be well lubricated with KY Jelly or some other preparation and should be inserted slowly and carefully, as the rectum is quite sensitive. Begin with a small amount of water (a pint or so). Over time, the slave will be able to hold more, although for practical cleanliness, no more than a quart is necessary. The "gallons and gallons" of water referred to in some pornographic literature should remain in the realm of fantasy.

If the slave suffers from hemorrhoids or rectal bleeding. or if these conditions develop at any point during training, she should inform the dominant, who must take great care not to aggravate the condition by requiring too-frequent cleansings. These common conditions can easily be treated by a health care professional.

The slave may also arrange her hair according to the dominant's wishes, use cosmetics (rouging the nipples and vulva, for example), trim or grow her nails, and so on. In all cases, such modifications should be undertaken, not out of vanity, but with the awareness of the dominant's wishes in mind.

# Control of the body

Some dominants take great pleasure in controlling the bodily functions of the slave. As long as such control does no damage to the slave's health, it is acceptable. Sade wrote a notorious passage in which he describes the ideal diet for a slave of a coprophiliac:

stewed chicken and rice. While Miss Abernathy does not condone the ingestion of feces, for reasons of hygiene and health, the concept of such intense bodily control is not unpleasant.

It is a sad fact that many submissives, so adept at caring for others, neglect their own well-being. Part of a dominant's task in training such a person is to instill good habits in matters of food, sleep, and exercise, and not to encourage self-destruction. If the dominant notices that the slave is remiss in matters of self-eare, he should take steps to remedy the situation. This can be accomplished from within the scene. For example, the dominant may wish to reward the slave for taking care of herself by allowing her to eat the same food as he does, perhaps leaving a little on his plate for the slave to enjoy. (Of course, she may be required to eat it without utensils while crouching on the floor.)

The dominant may also control the submissive's sleep, speech, and excretory functions, but great care should be taken not to exhaust the slave or endanger his health with such games.

The question of sexual abstinence for submissives frequently arises. Assuming that the slave has turned this right over to the dominant during negotiation, I believe that a dominant may act with impunity in restricting a slave's sexual pleasure. A state of sexual hunger drives slaves to better performance, and the promise of release is a powerful stimulant. If the dominant finds that the slave is unable to resist the temptation to masturbate, he may want to invest in one of the fine chastity belts or "cock cages" now available.

I am aware of no concrete evidence that sexual abstinence causes any problem other than frustration. Remind the slave that his sexual desire, like all else, is your property and should be dedicated to your pleasure, not the slave's.

**Forms of address.** In their speech, as in all else, slaves will find an opportunity to express their respect for the dominant. Most dominants will specify a default form of address, such as "Master" or "Mistress," "Sir" or "Madam." While in service, the slave should always use this honorific when addressing the dominant. If no default form is specified, the dominant should specify a form at the beginning of a training session, perhaps during the collaring ritual. He may say, "From this point on, you will address me as 'Master'." He shoudl expect the slave to reply, "Yes, Master." If such an acknowledgment is not forthcoming, he may prompt the slave. Dominants should be vigilant with forms of address; the slave should use it every time she addresses the dominant. Omissions should be noted and corrected. Nothing is more disappointing to a submissive than an inattentive dominant.

If a slave has become adept at one form of address, the dominant can up the ante by requiring a more complex form, such as the repetition of the honorific at the end of an utterance: "Master, may I please worship your boots now, Master?"

Honorifics can be simple or complex. They may or may not include a name. For example, a slave who is serving two masters, one to whom she is contracted and one who is only visiting the household, may address "her" master simply as "Master" and the other dominant by the honorific and his given name: "Master Jack."

An additional note on names is in order. Some dominants, especially professionals, use a "scene name" instead of or in addition to their legal or street name. Likewise, some submissives entering the community choose a scene name, and dominants may occasionally give their submissives "slave names." Individuals have diferent preferences regarding the use of scene names. I once heard a professional dominant at an S/M community function say, "Oh, please, call me [her given name]! We are all friends here; this is no dungeon."

Other professionals prefer to keep their given names private, for legal and personal reasons. When in doubt, ask. No one will fault you, and you will avoid awkward misunderstandings.

# Positioning the body

One of the most obvious ways that a slave can express his submission is through his body. A slave should strive to be graceful and unobtrusive at all times. Just as he should keep his mind focused on the task at hand, so he should eliminate unnecessary gestures.

The dominant should instruct the slave to assume a default posture when at rest. The most common postures are kneeling and standing. To assume the kneeling posture, the slave should fold his legs neatly beneath him. The knees may be held together or spread apart, according to the dominant's wishes. Hands may rest palm up or down on the thighs, may be clasped lightly at the small of the back, or the fingers may be laced behind the neck. The head should be inclined forward, the eyes cast down. Be aware that most Westerners are not accustomed to long periods of kneeling, so this posture may cause some discomfort. Slaves with existing knee problems should, of course, be given another posture to assume.

In the standing posture, for example, the slave stands erect with feet together or slightly apart. Hands are again clasped lightly behind the back, either at the base of the spine or at the waist, or they are left hanging loosely and gracefully at the sides. If the arms are at the sides, the slave should take care not to ball his hands into fists, but to let his open hand show his willingness to serve. Again, the head should be inclined and the eyes down. (In some exceptional cases, such as military training, the eyes may be kept up and forward.)

The slave should practice these postures under the direction of the dominant until he can execute them perfectly. He may then be shown "his" spot, the default location where he should assume the "at rest" posture when a task has been completed and he is awaiting further instruction.

In addition to the "at rest" posture, the slave should be made aware of any physical restrictions placed on him. Is he allowed to sit on the furniture? May he use utensils to eat? May he walk from place to place, or should he crawl? When, if ever, is it permissible to look the dominant in the eye? The dominant must reflect upon these details and inform the slave accordingly. Whatever the dominant's decision, she must be consistent. Unless her intent is to confuse and frustrate the slave, the dominant should stick to her own instructions when correcting a slave.

Many novice submissives find it difficult to hold still for any length of time. Often this has nothing to do with physical problems but indicates a lack of awareness of the body. Jiggling legs, tapping fingers, nervous coughs, and wandering eyes are to be discouraged. Instruct the submissive to focus his attention on his breathing and make a slow mental sweep along the full length of the body, taking note of any points of tension and relieving them. The submissive should also be instructed in basic stretches and encouraged to perform them regularly. This discipline will greatly increase a slave's capacity for maintaining postures.

Again, vigilance is paramount. Submissives expect correction and are often crushed when the dominant fails to notice an error. Such sloppiness undermines their confidence in the dominant and makes them question the sincerity of the dominant's commitment to them. The dominant's actions should always reinforce the slave's submission.

# Voice commands and postures

A slave should learn to respond immediately to verbal cornniands. Some commands are so frequent and simple that a word or two should elicit the desired effect. We have already covered the first two postures, kneeling and standing. Several more useful postures follow.

"**Come here.**" The dominant uses this command when ordering the slave to approach. The slave is expected to take the most direct route possible without disturbing any other people who may be in the area. She should either walk swiftly and gracefully to where the dominant is, or she should drop to her hands and knees and crawl there. Often the circumstances will dictate which method is appropriate. In a non-kinky setting, crawling will only cause scandal; likewise, a gravel path will damage the slave's knees or rip her clothing. When the slave reaches the dominant, she should stop within arm's reach and assume the "at rest" posture while waiting for further instruction.

She may also be expected to acknowledge the dominant verbally, as, for example, "You require me, Mistress?"

"**Go.**" This command is used when sending a slave to attend to a task or when the dominant wishes the slave to leave the room or area. The slave should again move quickly and gracefully. The key however, is to do so without turning his back on the dominant. Slaves must learn excellent observation skills: when entering a room, they should already be planning the most efficient way to exit it.

"**Follow**" or "**attend.**" This command tells the slave to follow the dominant as she moves about. Again, the slave is expected to crawl or to walk, although under most circumstances, walking is more efficient. When asked to "attend," the slave should be prepared to assist the dominant in other ways: by carrying packages, holding bags or drinks, fetching ashtrays or footstools, and a myriad of other small tasks.

"**Present.**" This command indicates that the slave should make her body available to the dominant in a pre-arranged fashion. The most common posture is kneeling with the legs spread wide and the pelvis tilted up, exposing the genitals. Hands should be lightly laced at the back of the neck, with elbows out to the sides. The shoulders should be thrown back to accentuate the breasts. Alternatively, the slave may be expected to kneel down on hands and knees, legs spread and head down, giving access to the posterior.

Another variation is "present for punishment." The dominant may also specify "present ass" or "present thighs" or whatever portion of the anatomy she intends as the recipient of her correction. Here the slave kneels down, pressing the top of the body flat against the ground and lifting the posterior into the air to receive the blows. Alternatively, he may lean across a table or other flat surface with his legs spread apart.

**"Open."** A related command is "open," upon which the slave should assume a position of sexual availability. The specifics of the posture depend upon the dominant's preferred way of using the slave. For women, this may mean a hands-and-knees posture like the second "present" option; stretched out on the back with legs spread; kneeling with mouth open; or bent over a convenient piece of furniture. For men, the hands-and-knees posture and the kneeling posture are appropriate for oral use; the slave may also be expected to lie on his back to be ridden.

**"Down" or "prostrate yourself."** Upon hearing this command, the slave should lie flat on his belly in front of the dominant. His arms should be stretched forward over his head and his feet should be pressed flat so the soles are exposed. The forehead should touch the floor. This posture may be used for abasement, confession, or as a prelude to worship.

**"Worship."** Here the slave should worship whatever object or body part the dominant offers. Worship is generally understood to be oral, using both lips and tongue, unless otherwise specified. Worship should always be respectful, never greedy or sloppy.

Nothing is more offensive than a slave who drools on
slobbers on a dominant's hand. Consider that the lips a
express the totality of the slave's devotion during worship. Sometimes
a dominant will allow the slave to cradle the object or body part in
his hands, or will rest it on his shoulder, as when a Mistress rests her
booted leg on a slave's shoulder to allow better access to the top of
the boot or to her sex.

# Basic forms of service for slaves

In addition to being able to execute the basic positions described
in the previous section, slaves should be able to perform some
basic tasks. Not all of the tasks listed are appropriate for every type
of slave; dominants can pick and choose at their discretion.

**Housework**. The amount and type of housework a
dominant may require will vary with the dominant's living
situation and personal standards of tidiness. Whether she lives
in a small apartment or a cavernous mansion, the dominant will
need the following:

- floors swept and washed (and possibly polished)
- rugs vacuumed and possibly cleaned
- surfaces and objects dusted
- counters cleaned
- dishes washed, dried, and put away
- laundry washed, dried, folded or ironed, and put away
- simple meals and beverages prepared

If the dominant has specifications for any of these tasks –
whether socks are to be folded or balled, the proper proportions
of sugar and milk in tea, which china to use for guests and which
for everyday – she must make them very clear to the slave, or
she will be disappointed. Slaves, for their part, ought always to

ask how to do a task if they are unsure, rather than doing it incorrectly and wasting their own time and the dominant's by having to do it again. It is also the dominant's responsibility to provide the necessary tools and supplies for any household cleaning task.

**Errands.** Almost everyone has at some time wished that the groceries would magically appear in the cupboard. Slaves should be prepared to do basic grocery and sundry shopping for the dominant. In preparing a shopping list, the slave should note the dominant's preferred brands and should inquire about specialty items like coffee, tea, chocolate, liquor, and unusual bath products. The dominant should make arrangements to pay for the goods in some simple way – a presigned check, an ATM card from a household account, or cash. The slave may be expected to shop within a budget, and efforts toward economy should be rewarded.

A slave can do many other simple errands: dropping off and picking up dry cleaning (be sure to provide the slave with the claim check ticket); going to the post office and retrieving the dominant's mail and packages from a post office box or mail drop (make sure the slave has the key or make arrangements with the postmaster in advance); returning rented items, such as videos or cars; picking up forms at the DMV or insurance companies. Remember that many large cities have droves of "professional organizers" who make their living running errands for busy people. Your slave is a valuable resource.

If the slave will be driving, she should be able to produce a valid driver's license, registration, and proof of insurance for her vehicle. If the slave will be using the dominant's vehicle, be sure the insurance covers other drivers. The slave should be responsible for any parking or traffic tickets incurred, and

should be firmly chastised for such irresponsible beh
in fact gets one.

**Personal attendance.** A slave should be ready to fetch
and carry the dominant's possessions or to deliver messages to
third parties. The dominant should instruct the slave in basic
grooming and clothing care, and may expect the slave to trim or
style her hair, provide her with a manicure or pedicure, or even
apply her makeup. Slaves are often responsible for drawing baths
and attending the dominant while she bathes. The slave should
be able to press clothing and do any basic mending – hemming,
buttons, and the like – that may be necessary. If the dominant
wears leather shoes or boots, the slave should know how to clean
and polish them.

**Sexual techniques.** If the slave has been engaged for
sexual use, he should be trained to perform whatever type of
sexual service the dominant most enjoys. A sex slave should
always be prepared to be used, and should make sure that the
necessary supplies – condoms, latex gloves, lubricant, and such
– are at hand. This may mean carrying a supply on his person,
or secreting caches away around the house. Spontaneity is
no excuse for unsafe sex. Nor should the dominant allow his
demands to endanger the slave or himself. As one dominant of
my acquaintance is fond of saying, "If you break your toys, you
don't get to play with them anymore."

**Special skills.** Any of the basic skills described above can
become the focus of a slave's training. A simple maid may become
an expert in household management and advance to the position
of housekeeper. Similarly, a slave who shows a talent for personal
care might be sent to study massage or hairdressing. Sex slaves
can train in techniques of special interest to the dominant, such
as fisting or Tantric breath. A slave who shows a special talent in

the kitchen can train as a chef. Open schools like The Learning Annex offer many classes for a nominal fee, from wine-tasting to stripping, that the dominant may wish the slave to attend. Copies of any certificates or transcripts from such classes should be duly added to the slave's file.

**Voice-training.** Voice-training is a specialized area of accomplishment that many slaves never approach. At its simplest, voice-training involves teaching a slave when it is appropriate to maintain silence (which is most of the time) and when and how to speak. This type of training is usually part of any basic program. In its more advanced form, voice-training requires practice in reading or recitation or other types of vocal performance, and is useful for slaves expected to entertain at social functions. It may also refer to training a slave to respond to dominants in away that avoids references to the self or to the slave's own preferences or will. Responses such as "If it pleases you, Sir," or "Whatever Mistress wishes," fall into this category. In its most advanced form, voice-training may include instruction in foreign languages and complex social etiquette, and is appropriate for slaves who will act as escorts or companions to diplomats or businesspeople or who show a special aptitude for and interest in languages. Advanced voice-training requires a commitment of many years and is best reserved for long-term contracts.

# Punishment

It is inevitable that at some point in her training, even the most accomplished slave will make a mistake. The dominant should set clear guidelines for correction of errors. If the point of the punishment is correction, then the rule is, "Let the punishment fit the crime." In general, errors that indicate lack of consideration for the dominant or behavior that runs counter to the agreed-upon code of ethics for the slave should be punished more severely than simple physical mistakes. Errors of the former sort include the following: neglecting proper forms of address, disobeying direct commands, gossiping, arrogance, tardiness, failure to complete a training assignment, disrespect in any form.

Punishments should also suit the slave. A slave who is very attached to a token may have that token taken away for a period of time. A slave who consistently forgets honorifics may be put under a discipline of total silence; this technique is also useful for gossips. Arrogant slaves may be denied use of the furniture or eating utensils. A slave who is unduly proud of his appearance may be dressed in unfashionable or ill-fitting clothes or be denied access to the bath. In extreme cases, the dominant may choose to send the slave away for a period of time. Miss Abernathy believes this punishment should be reserved for only the most obdurate slaves or for when the dominant feels unable to control her own anger.

In more simple cases, repetition is the key. If a slave cannot remember how to fold the dominant's socks, it may be time for her to empty the entire sock drawer and refold every pair correctly. If a slave forgets to use the lower-case "i" in written assignments, she may be required to write "i must be humble," one hundred times. Slaves who lose keys or bus passes may be made to wear them around their necks on a string, like schoolchildren do. Never underestimate the power of humiliation.

Physical discipline may prove useful for slaves who are physically and psychically able to withstand it. Often the mere threat of a beating is enough to whip the slave into shape. A petulant, whining submissive slave should be taken over the dominant's knee and spanked like the child he is. A slave who is negligent in his use of honorifics can be required to count each stroke, thanking the dominant in appropriately respectful form. Lazy slaves who are caught sitting around may be paddled so that when they next sit down, their bruises will remind them of their obligations.

Dominants sometimes find themselves at a loss about how to punish masochistic slaves, for whom physical beatings are the purest pleasure. One method is to deny the slave a beating or administer one with a tool that the slave does not enjoy. Another tactic is to use some other form of punishment, such as memorizing a humiliatingly silly poem, or performing some seemingly endless task, like scrubbing the bathroom grout with bleach and a toothbrush. The slave might also be asked to perform a particularly challenging task, as a chance to turn the punishment into an occasion for reward.

# Recognition and reward

Just as a slave's deficiencies must be corrected, her achievements should be duly noted and rewarded. Rewards may be physical – a sensuous beating for a masochist, an orgasm for a sex slave – or material, such as a token or a new uniform.

**Privilege: the best reward of all.** The simplest and often most effective form of reward is privilege. A slave who is allowed greater intimacy with the dominant and a more advanced level of service will feel treasured as the valuable possession he is. Once again, the reward should fit the slave. For a fetishist, worshipping the fetish object to his heart's content may be in order. Likewise, permission to entertain the dominant by masturbating in front of him would be an excellent reward for a slave who has shown exemplary sexual restraint. If the slave is a "switch," that is, if he has dominant tendencies as well as submissive, one great reward may be the gift of his own slave to train.

# The collar

The slave collar remains the most widely recognized mark of submission. As such, it makes an excellent reward for a new slave who has completed her preparations well. One dominant friend of mine has devised a collar system. As his slave progresses through the training program, she is rewarded with different collars, each representing a new level of achievement: first white, then red, then green and so on. (Another dominant might provide medals or badges with appropriate titles. Dominants with a military bent may mark each advance in rank with a "stripe.")

Many slaves crave the collar; some can barely function without it. When a dominant collars her slave, she signals that their roles are in full effect. By accepting the collar, the slave indicates her willingness to serve the dominant at that time. If the collaring is performed publicly, at a play party or other community function, it alerts other players that the slave is unavailable and that the dominant should be approached before any contact is made with the slave.

Collars may be of many different types, from the studded black leather variety to a simple velvet ribbon. Dominants must take great care in selecting the collar, for it is a tangible symbol of their will and their commitment to the slave. The collar should suit the slave's role. A choke-chain is appropriate for a slave submitting to canine training, a delicate lace ribbon may adorn a lady's maid. Submissives who serve in non-kinky public should be provided with a more subtle collar, a stylish silver chain from a jeweler's or even a length of leather lacing in the dominant's signature color – to avoid undue attention and confrontation with potentially hostile outsiders. (The submissive may of course be given a more formal collar for service in the home or at BDSM functions.)

Miss Abernathy has a particular prejudice regarding collars: they should lock. Anyone may wear a collar for casual play or for the sheer fashion value of it, but a submissive in service to a dominant should be given the assurance that a locked collar provides. The lock not only holds the submissive captive to the dominant, but binds the dominant to the submissive. A dominant may wish to display the key as a pendant to remind the slave and any onlookers of her power and love for the submissive. (One note of caution is in order here: all locks should have more than one working key, and the submissive should be informed of the location of an emergency key and the specific circumstances under which he may use it to release himself from the collar. I am speaking of real emergencies here: fire, earthquakes, medical crises.)

Collars should fit snugly without impeding movement or restricting breathing. One exception is the posture collar, which is designed to hold the neck straight and the head forward. They are especially useful for slouching sissy maids or other servants who lack focus. A posture collar should be fitted by a knowledgeable leatherworker to assure that it does not damage the neck, restrict breathing, or chafe the skin. Many dominants prefer adjustable collars, particularly if the slave is expected to do heavy labor or to sleep in the collar. In both cases, the neck may swell, and loosening the collar a notch will prevent the danger of strangulation.

**The collaring ritual.** When being collared, the slave should present herself in a manner that displays her gratitude and willingness to serve. Miss Abernathy prefers a kneeling position with the head inclined, eyes cast downward, and palms resting lightly on the thighs. If the slave is presenting the collar, she should hold it in her upturned hands and, raising her arms above her head, offer it to the dominant, who should not have to bend or stretch to reach it. The dominant may then command the slave to "kneel up" to receive the collar. At this command, the slave rises so that the body forms a straight line from neck to knees. She should raise her head enough to allow the dominant to encircle her neck with the collar.

At this point, the dominant may require the slave to make some gesture of gratitude, such as kissing the collar, reciting a pledge of service, or simply requesting sincerely that the dominant collar her. Then the dominant will put the collar around the slave's neck, perhaps expressing its significance to her and to the slave: "While you wear this collar, you are mine to command. You will obey me without hesitation. And as long as you wear it, I will consider you my responsibility. I will let no harm come to you as long as you are in my care." The dominant may at this time specify her preferred form of address, any tasks the slave is to perform, and any specific disciplines the slave may be under, such as not using utensils to eat or remaining silent.

Submissives, take note: although you may wear it for years, do not make the mistake of thinking that the collar belongs to you. Unless he specifically indicates otherwise, the collar remains the property of the dominant and must therefore be returned immediately upon request. Should the slave choose to lay aside the collar without warning or explanation, the dominant may reasonably assume that the slave has broken contract and no longer wishes to be in service. Naturally, such gestures made without prior communication are likely to cause confusion and hurt feelings and are best avoided. In the matter of collars, as in all things, both the dominant and the submissive are obligated to express themselves as clearly and directly as possible at all times.

# Ornaments or tokens

In addition to the collar, the dominant may wish to reward the slave by providing any number of different types of tokens for the slave to wear. Some leather shops make customized brass, silver, or leather name plates, which can be worn on a jacket, attached to the collar itself, or otherwise displayed on the slave's clothing. Dog tags, both of the military and canine varieties, can be embossed with owner's name, address, and so on. Jewelers can engrave similar information on ID bracelets, rings, or most charming, ankle bracelets, those lovely remnants of shackles. Tokens can be even more subtle. The dominant may require the slave to wear a signature color or to carry a handkerchief impregnated with the dominant's perfume or cologne. Such intimate items provide solace to a slave temporarily separated from her owner. In any case, the token should serve as a constant reminder of servitude.

# Permanent marks

Other slaves may literally earn their stripes: permanent marks to show their accomplishments in the service arts. Just as O first earned the "irons" (labia piercings) and later a brand, a dominant can reward a slave with ornamental body modifications. Such marks represent a deep commitment and should never be undertaken lightly.

It should go without saying that no one ought to be marked without his or her explicit permission. No reputable professional will mark an unwilling person, and neither should a dominant.

The most common forms of permanent marks in D/S relationships are piercings, brands, cuttings, and tattoos.

**Piercing.** Permanent body piercing has become very stylish in the past few years, with the rich and famous sporting nose, nipple, and navel piercings. For a dominant to give a submissive rings, however, the relationship should be more than a seasonal fashion. Any kind of permanent piercing can have significance as a dominant's mark, but the most common piercings are earlobe, nipple, and genital. The earlobe is convenient, visible, and socially acceptable. Marking may be as simple as the submissive wearing an earring purchased by or belonging to the dominant. The surgical stainless steel rings commonly used at piercing salons can be adorned with a bead in the dominant's signature color. A small engraved pendant with the dominant's initials can be hung from an earring.

Nipple piercings are distinctly more erotic (for most people!) than earlobe piercings. Sensitivity often increases when a nipple is pierced; also, the nipple spreads. Nipple skin is tough, and provided the piercing is well-healed and the jewelry sturdy enough, pierced nipples can take a lot of stimulation. A sadistic dominant may use this state to her advantage. It may also amuse her to lead her slave around a party by a leash attached to his nipple jewelry or to hang an engraved pendant or weight from it.

Genital piercings are certainly the most highly erotically charged piercings. Not only do most genital piercings increase erotic sensation, but piercing a slave's genitals sends a very definite message: this is mine. O's irons were labia piercings ornamented with her master's initials, but almost any part of the female or male external genitalia can be pierced: the clitoral hood, inner and outer labia, the penis head and shaft, the scrotal sac, the perineum.

*Do not try to pierce your slave yourself! All piercings should be done by trained individuals only!!* The popularity of piercing has resulted in many fly-by-night piercers (and dominants) who have only a few days or weeks of training. It is better to go without the piercing until you can schedule an appointment with a reputable piercer than to risk infection and worse.

Piercings have the advantage that they are practical (in S/M terms), they are beautiful, and if the jewelry is removed, they will usually heal over (although rarely without some sort of scar). In the event that the relationship ends, the submissive will not be left with a large or obvious mark that reminds her of her loss every time she sees it.

**Other permanent marks.** The same cannot be said for branding, tattooing, or cutting.

While all three have intense erotic associations – O was branded, after all – they are potentially dangerous procedures that, like piercing, should be done by trained individuals only. Some established body modification artists will be happy to perform bonding rituals between a dominant and submissive that center on marking.

In choosing a design for a brand, tattoo, or cutting, a dominant should bear in mind that the submissive may well wear it for the rest of her life. Symbols that are too intimately connected to the dominant – names, initials, portraits –make poor choices. It is much better to choose a symbol of commitment or of transformation, such as a circular Celtic knot or a phoenix. Totem animals or runes are another good choice, since they invoke protection. The dominant may want to explore the art of the slave's particular ethnic group(s) in deciding on a design.

# Testing

The dominant may sometimes feel it necessary to test the slave. She may doubt the slave's sincerity or she may want to assess the level of his development in specific skills. In either case, she may choose to create a situation in which the slave will be asked to prove his obedience, honesty, skill, or devotion. If a slave has been studying tea service, the easiest way to test his skill is to invite several trusted friends over for afternoon tea. To test a slave's obedience, ask him to perform a seemingly humiliating or dangerous task (the danger need not even be real). To prove a slave's honesty, ask a friend to tell the slave something unpleasant – perhaps a critique of the dominant's behavior – and then make the slave recount the conversation. Slaves prove their love and devotion at every turn, in the small acts of service that make up their day, but loyalty in times of trouble is the best measure of a slave's devotion.

The principles of testing should be discussed in a theoretical way during preliminary negotiations and consent received. Particularly in the case of a "set-up," like the test of honesty described above, tests may involve mild deceptions, and if the dominant does not admit them, he cannot reasonably expect his slaves to admit their deceptions either.

# Other types of service

**Public attendance and play**. Thus far we have spoken mainly of private service in the home. For many dominants and slaves, this will be the extent of their interaction. For those people who live in areas with an active BDSM community, or who have like-minded friends, public service and play can form a large part of their relationship.

**Escorting.** A dominant may require her slave to escort her to various social functions, such as parties, theater performances, and the like. These situations give the slave a chance to perfect and display her social graces and poise. Public attendance can be extraordinarily challenging, especially for submissives who are accustomed to private service. The noise and bustle, the numerous chance encounters with strangers and friends, and the simple desire to do well can overwhelm a slave. Dominants should take time to acknowledge the slave's performance, either during or after the event.

Here a note on discretion is in order. There are relatively few public situations in which a dominant and slave can appear as they are – as owner and property. While Miss Abernathy believes that pride and confidence in one's life choices are laudable, she nevertheless cautions against inappropriate displays that may lead to conflict and confrontation. Taking your slave to The Four Seasons on a leash is not recommended. Neither is requiring obviously submissive behavior in front of a slave's professional colleagues, if such behavior would damage her credibility. Parents may still have their children removed from their care if their BDSM lifestyle becomes public. How much is public display worth to you?

**Lending slaves out.** If a dominant and his slave are part of the larger BDSM community in their area, they may wish to open their relationship to friends and other players. Very often this will take the form of lending the slave out. The slave may be sent to another top for discipline or to perform some special service, or may be engaged to help train a less experienced submissive in what may be called a "middle" position. If the slave has abduction or "gang" fantasies, the dominant may wish to arrange a group scene as a special treat. The dominant should take special care to inform the other players of the slaves interests and limitations and should observe the entire procedure carefully to ensure the slave's safety.

A special case is the slave auction. Most major American cities have social clubs and events for BDSM aficionados, where dominants and submissives can be open about their relationships and tastes. One favored event is the slave auction. Here a slave (or an unattached submissive) is put on the block and "sold" to the highest bidder. Often what is being auctioned is not the slave *in toto*, but "first negotiation rights" or a specific skill of the slave's, such as boot polishing or massage or cooking.

Group scenes do bring up the matter of jealousy, and it would be unwise to ignore it. Dominant/submissive relationships are by definition possessive, and it is not uncommon for a dominant to resent the attention his slave pays to another dominant (even if it has been negotiated) or for a slave to feel wounded at the sight of "her" dominant with another. Miss Abernathy's advice is "Know thyself." If you are a naturally jealous person, admit it. If you prefer a monogamous relationship, do not settle for anything else; you will only be miserable. There are dominants who find the idea of their slave serving anyone else appalling, there are certainly slaves who are happiest when focused on one person and one person only. Nowhere does it say that all BDSM players must be non-monogamous, although many are happily (and ethically) so. Choosing this lifestyle means choosing to live as you see fit, regardless of society's qualms. Do not then fall prey to another set of arbitrary rules.

# Tools and accoutrements for training

**Clothing.** The clothing a dominant chooses for a slave should suit both the dominant's personal tastes and the practical requirements of the slave's position. It is ridiculous to ask a butler to wear a maid's uniform (except as a form of humiliating punishment) or to require a sex slave to be bundled up from head to toe.

In general, there are two schools of slave couture. The first believes that slaves should be naked at all times. This option is most practical for slaves who serve exclusively in the dominant's home or at play parties and is especially appealing for sex slaves. A slave may perform many tasks around the home while naked and not suffer any ill effects. (Two tasks that should be avoided are cleaning with caustic chemicals and cooking.)

The second school holds that slaves ought to be outfitted with a uniform appropriate to their status. A sissy maid should never be without stockings and gaff (an undergarment used to conceal male genitalia); a butler, without a dark formal suit. Sex slaves can also be outfitted in appealing lingerie or scanty skirts or loincloths that leave them physically accessible to the dominant at all times. Any slave who is engaged for sexual service should be prepared to strip down on command.

It is vital that the dominant provide adequate clothing for specific tasks. A slave who gardens should be given gloves and knee pads as well as the necessary tools for her work. If the slave has particularly sensitive skin, she should be given lined rubber gloves before being asked to wash dishes or scrub the toilet. It is appropriate, as part of the slave's training, to require a list of all the necessary "tools of the trade" for any given role or task. It is the dominant's responsibility to provide these items, unless other arrangements have been made.

Many slaves find that costumes or uniforms or the experience of forced nakedness trigger their submission. Likewise, dominants may find that certain articles of clothing – boots, a corset, a leather vest – put them in a more dominant frame of mind... and excite the submissive. If the slave has a fetish, the dominant may wish to indulge that fetish, or she may wish to save it for a special reward. Although a slave should be ready and willing to serve a Mistress who is weanng tennis shoes and sweatpants, both parties may want to experiment with costuming as an added perk.

**Hidden items.** Many slaves benefit from the judicious use of "hidden" training devices that can be worn under street clothes. The transvestite maid who spends his days in an office may find the caress of a pair of silky panties or fine nylon stockings under his suit just the thing to help him through the day and prepare him for his evening chores. Sissy maids may be required to wear a gaff to disguise the male genitals, and a dominant may wish a slave to wear it on a daily basis. This form of training is especially efficacious if the maid is required to shop for the items himself, in, say, an exclusive boutique or at Victoria's Secret.

A dominant may also require the slave to wear a corset or waist-training belt under her work clothes. It is imperative that such items not restrict the slave's movement or respiration so severely as to interfere with her work or her health. A hidden item should be a constant, gentle reminder of the dominant and of the slave's status.

Some dominants favor the use of anal insertion devices ("butt plugs") in their training programs. Butt plugs, which are available in a wide variety of shapes, materials and sizes, are particularly beneficial for sex slaves of anally inclined masters and mistresses. They may also be used a punishment, although again, they should not interfere with the slave's ability to function in the workplace and should not damage his body. Therefore, plugs should not be left in place for more than a few minutes to start. The time may be increased to several hours as the slave adjusts. The anus can be stretched with increasingly large butt plugs, so that it may later accommodate other items, like a large penis, a latex-sheathed whip handle, or several gloved fingers.

Female slaves whose masters wish to train them for more active sexual service may wish them to "pack" – that is, to wear a strap-on dildo under their regular clothing. This technique is also useful for gender-switching women who serve as "boys." There exists an underground literature – these days transmitted by way of the Internet – on the fine art of packing. Dildos, like butt plugs, come in a variety of shapes, sizes and materials, from soft "herbies" (sometimes called "pants-fillers") to superhuman dongs. The slave can stuff a small, soft dildo in her underwear – men's Y-fronts or a jockstrap are appropriate choices – or can use a harness with larger toys. Harnesses are usually made either of durable but soft leather, or of webbing. The former has the benefit of high fetish value; the latter is easier to clean, lighter in weight, and less expensive. The slave should be instructed in the proper care of both dildo and harness and should learn the advantages of different styles of underwear and trousers, the merits of condoms (and their use) and the most pleasing way to handle "her dick." Pornography featuring male-male scenes may form an important part of her education.

# S/M tools

Not all submissives are masochists and not all dominants are sadists. In the event that this happy convergence of tastes occurs, however, the dominant may wish to acquire and use tools designed for S/M play. Physical sensation can be used as a punishment or as a reward. Choose your "weapon" well: trainers may prefer a leather strap while a governess may reach for a fine rattan cane. A canine trainer may prefer a rolled-up newspaper; the equestrienne, a crop. Or the dominant may choose to make her open hand a tool: a firm swat on the behind makes a fine choice as reward or punishment.

# Part Two: D/S Relationships

---

**In which we explore the nature and logistics of dominant/submissive arrangements from the acquisition of slaves to the negotiation of contracts.**

---

Perhaps you are a dominant looking for a slave. How on earth do you find one? You could look to that capricious mistress, Fate, to deliver your future property to your doorstep, but burnt offerings or no, the Goddess has a backlog of requests for happiness, so you would do well to consider more mundane options.

Many people have successfully found partners through personal ads in their local alternative papers, Usenet newsgroups, or specialized websites such as alt.com, bondage.com or adultfriendfinder.com. A number of excellent books can give you tips on finding partners (see the Bibliography for suggestions).

In addition to advertising and "cruising" the Internet, many dominants and submissives enjoy the support and stimulation of BDSM organizations. Most major American cities boast several such organizations; some, like New York's TES and San Francisco's Society of Janus and Exiles, have existed for many years. Most organizations offer educational workshops and social events for their membership; some host BDSM play parties; many publish on-line and/or print newsletters. Joining one of these organizations and attending BDSM parties, conferences, contests, and events are certainly the most direct methods of meeting compatible individuals.

How do you signal your interest in D/S? The lesbian and gay leather communities have their hanky codes: a bandanna displayed on the left by tops, on the right by bottoms, with every color of the rainbow signifying a particular activity or fetish. I have yet to see a hanky that signified dominance or submission, however, although some, like white lace for Victorian scenes, can be adapted for that use. Other writers and craftspeople have suggested rings (such as a reproduction of the ring worn by the dominants in *Story of O),* bracelets or anklets, or other trinkets.

My suggestion is this: wear whatever suits you and let your manner speak for you. By this I do not mean that dominants should be indiscriminately haughty; this is rudeness, not dominance. Nor do I advise submissives to throw themselves willy-nilly at the feet of dominants. Such behavior is disrespectful, both to the dominant and to the submissive himself. An attitude of quiet, attentive grace suits a submissive better than wanton gestures of abasement. Likewise, an observant and controlled manner conveys dominance more readily than pushiness or obnoxious, egocentric displays of "power."

# What to look for in a submissive

Beyond mere availability and erotic compatibility, what qualities should a dominant look for in a potential slave? Here Miss Abernathy must admit to a certain prejudice. For many dominants, the intellectual acumen of a slave and his or her spiritual development are relatively unimportant. Not so for me. I am simply uninterested in a slave with whom I cannot carry on a lively conversation. In fact, my personal list of required qualities begins with "highly verbal." Clearly, certain roles require specific skills: it would be foolish to employ a cook who burns water. Half the pleasure of owning a slave is in the training, however – so if what you want is only a cook, call an agency and hire a cook. If what you want is an accomplished chef who has a foot fetish or who can recite Yeats while being caned or who is willing and able to learn French so that she can accompany you to the film festival at Cannes, that is a slave.

In general, though, I believe that all slaves should exhibit some basic qualities. A slave should be sincere, loyal, discreet, clean, modest, honest, graceful, intelligent (that is, able to learn what is required for her position), respectful of herself and others, observant, attentive, and ethical.

In addition to these basic qualities, a dominant may require other characteristics, such as physical attractiveness, strength or stamina, specific sexual traits, a pleasant voice (particularly important for slaves to be voice-trained), social adaptability, or specific technical skills (construction, sewing, writing, accounting and the like).

I would like to say a word about a particular phenomenon that may arise between submissive and dominant. You will remember, no doubt, the urgency with which Severin pursued his Mistress, Wanda, in *Venus In Furs*. What you may not recall is her initial reluctance to fulfill his fantasy. It is possible to read *Venus In Furs* as the story of a would-be slave who is submissive only to his own fantasies. Gregor (as Severin was called while in service to his lady) is a textbook example of a pushy submissive who "tops from the bottom." I do not wish to imply that a real-life submissive should have no input into a contract or the ways in which it is carried out, but there is a qualitative difference between a dominant who enters into a contract freely – who indeed will most often initiate it – and one who is bullied into adopting a "dominant" position by a needy submissive. Gregor created a monster in Wanda, one with whom he quickly became dissatisfied. I refer to the tendency to bully people into dominance as "Gregor Syndrome"; individuals afflicted with it should be avoided.

# To those who would be masters...

**Personal qualities of a good dominant.** Just as a slave must exhibit exemplary qualities, so must a dominant show that he is worthy of the privilege of ownership. Just because a person is a sexual "top" or sadist does not automatically mean that he will be a good dominant.

First and foremost, the dominant should possess at least the same level of personal integrity that he expects from his slave. While "do as I say, not as I do" may be an amusing erotic game, it cannot, in the long run, form the basis of a dominant/submissive arrangement.

Second, the dominant should have a clear sense of his own limitations and needs, and be able to articulate them clearly and succinctly. A dominant must have exceptionally good personal boundaries, particularly since slavehood implies a level of dependence on the dominant.

Third, a dominant should be inquisitive. The best dominants are insatiably curious about human nature. This curiosity drives such individuals to dig deep into the hearts and minds of submissives to discover what makes them tick. A dominant must be highly observant – nosy, even. Selective prying is the dominant's prerogative.

A dominant should be creative, versatile, and decisive, both in matters of reward and of punishment. The tasks she sets for her submissive, the authority with which she presents new restraints and challenges, the ingenuity with which she approaches the training process – all these are vital if the dominant wishes to avoid boredom and conventionality in her relationships.

I believe that a dominant should herself have an intimate knowledge of the tasks she sets for a submissive. So, while she need not be physically able to do a task herself, she should both understand the logistics of the problem and appreciate the skill and energy necessary to complete it. Not only does this assure that the dominant will value the slave appropriately, but it will also allow her to the better correct the slave in the event of an error or insufficiency in the work. A dominant must be both teacher and student, able to learn from her peers and from her slaves.

This raises the broader question of nature versus nurture. Are the best dominants born, or are they made? Old School wisdom has it that the best tops start at the bottom; that is, that a would-be dominant should undergo training as a submissive in order to appreciate the complexities of service. To the extent that this is possible, given the resources of the community and the individual's temperament, I think it is sound advice. Certainly there are those who are constitutionally unsuited for submission, and I am not suggesting that such individuals force themselves into an unnatural role. To them I recommend extensive observation of successful D/S relationships, and, if possible, the experience of co-topping or co-owning a submissive. Indeed, some of the most successful masters have been trained by slaves or by more experienced dominants in exactly this manner.

Just as submissives can suffer from "Gregor Syndrome," dominants are prone to a number of ailments as well. The most general is known as "top's disease," or, in common parlance, delusions of grandeur. Just because you are suzy slave's master doesn't mean you are automatically Master of the Universe. It is inappropriate and downright rude to try to dominate innocent bystanders; in some cases, this behavior can become abusive.

A related ailment is "Wanda Syndrome," named after Gregor's mistress in *Venus In Furs*. A dominant suffering from Wanda Syndrome is actually letting herself be dominated by her so-called submissive. Often this leads to resentment, and, in some cases, betrayal and abandonment, as was the case in Sacher-Masoch's novel. Passive-aggressive behavior and codependency are as unhealthy in a dominant/submissive relationship as in any other.

**Commitment and resources.** Just as slavehood can be a vocation, responsible and committed dominance can be a source of great joy and satisfaction. However, in the desire to possess and care for a submissive, some dominants overestimate their own level of commitment and resources. If you are having trouble paying your own rent, it is foolish to take on a live-in slave. If you are a naturally monogamous person, contracting with a submissive whose greatest fantasy is to be lent out to your friends would be a grave error.

One dominant of my acquaintance has written, "The Mistress must be worthy of the servant." I can only applaud her. I believe that the best dominants are essentially modest. A modest dominant is not an oxymoron. She must know her limits and her weaknesses as well as her strong points; how else can she dare to correct someone else's? She does not suffer from delusions of grandeur or overestimate her abilities. She does not believe herself to be a panacea for the world's ills, and especially not for a submissive's inner pain. No one, but no one, can "cure" another person's childhood wounds or spiritual malaise. At best, a dominant can help create a supportive atmosphere in which to allow a submissive to heal those wounds herself.

**Styles of dominance.** Just as there is a wide variety of submissives, dominants do not come in one flavor only. There are the classic roles of *mistress* and *master*. (It should be noted that masters may be female or male. Some women prefer the title *mastress*. I suppose that there may also be male mistresses, although I do not know any personally.) The archetypal mistress is a leather goddess wearing towering spike-heeled boots; she is wasp-waisted in her corset and brandishes a whip. Yet how many women are inclined to prance around their homes in clothing that is more like bondage than any chains? Very few, in my experience. More often, "mistress" is a general title of respect for a dominant woman, whatever her style. Likewise, a master may be macho in his chaps and mirrored shades – or a friendly gentleman in a business suit. *Nota bene:* just as a submissive may well be offended by a random individual trying to "top" her, many dominants dislike being addressed as "master" or "mistress" without prior negotiation, even in a kink-friendly environment.

The key aspect of a mistress or master is authority, and especially authority based on personal achievement. We speak of a master craftsperson or of a Master of Arts degree. In both of these cases, the tide of "master" is conferred after years of training and work. Likewise in D/S, the title of master or mistress ought to be earned, not taken.

Another role is that of the *trainer*. Trainers often model themselves after athletic, military, or animal trainers; they are often primarily concerned with performance. The trainer is the natural complement to the pet; a butler in the middle position of supervising other slaves may also act as a trainer.

An *owner* can be a master, trainer, or mistress; here the emphasis is on the submissive as possession. Owners are suitable dominants for pets and for slaves who enjoy being first and foremost someone's property.

A final category of dominant is the *teacher*. In this group we find governesses, headmasters and -mistresses, the Mother Superior and the local priest. In all cases, the dominant stands *in loco parentis,* assuming a disciplinary pseudo-parental role. A teacher may also take on a dominant-in-training. In any case, one would expect a teacher to have a particular area of expertise, be it French or fencing.

# To those who would be slaves...

While this book is primarily addressed to dominants, I have no doubt that some submissives will have braved their way through it as well. If you are one of these, you are to be commended... but also forewarned. It takes more than good posture and pretty manners to make a slave. I must repeat myself: slavehood is a vocation. It requires patience, hard work, unflinching honesty, and a strong sense of self. The following short essay will, I trust, give you food for thought on your journey.

# On ethics

Miss Abernathy strongly believes that our world and our community cries out for a more balanced and harmonious ethical structure, one that ends neither in an eye-for-an-eye literalism nor in a turn-the-other-cheek denial of the self. I find in medieval chivalry an embodiment of such a system. The following pages do not contain a lengthy discussion of chivalry as a historical and literary phenomenon. Rather, I have taken the terminology of chivalric ethics as a starting point for a discussion of submission and service.

While this section is addressed primarily to submissives, I hope it wilt become apparent that these guidelines represent an ethical structure appropriate to dominants as well.

**Foundations of submissive ethics.** In his romance *Lancelot (The Knight of the Cart)*, the twelfth-century French poet Chrétien de Troyes tells the story of a famous knight in service to a famous queen. Lancelot has vowed to do his lady's will without hesitation, thinking not of himself but only of her wishes. One day, the queen requires Lancelot to climb into a cart – which, the author tells us, was used in those times like a pillory, to display common criminals to public mockery. The proud knight, forgetting his vow, hesitates for the space of two steps, and the queen rebukes him, causing him no end of distress. When the two finally meet again, he asks why she has ignored him, her faithful lover.

Then the queen explains to him:

> *"What? Were you not then ashamed and afraid of the cart? You showed great reluctance to climb in when you hesitated for the pace of two steps. That indeed was why I refused either to address you or to look at you." "May God save me," says Lancelot, "from doing such a wrong a second time; and may God never have mercy on me if you are not absolutely right![...]"* (trans. D.D.R. Owen)

What kind of a relationship is this, where one partner may ask the other to humiliate himself publicly for her sake? Courtly love, although it is the source of many of our modern notions of romantic love, diverges sharply from its contemporary counterpart in that love is explicitly defined in terms of the lover's service to his lady. The relationship is one of fealty, a vow of devotion to an individual and commitment to serving him or her. Such was a knight's vow to his king, and such is that same knight's vow to his lady love.

The unattainable woman. The devoted lover. Seemingly random acts of disdain that humiliate the lover. His continued adoration and increased fervor. We might just as easily be reading Sacher-Masoch's *Venus In Furs* as a medieval romance. Just as Gregor submits to the humiliation of traveling as Wanda's servant, riding in crowded, smelly coaches with the commoners and sleeping in cold and drafty servant's quarters, Lancelot, the flower of chivalry, submits to the punishment of the cart: the mark of the common, the mean. And all for love.

What qualities did a chivalrous lover possess? What did he offer his lady in return for her affection? And how can a modern submissive interpret and adapt this seemingly archaic system to his own situation? What does it really mean to love, honor, and obey?

**Friendship.** I believe that no dominant/submissive relationship can exist without the bonds of mutual affection. I am not talking about a casual affair or mere erotic titillation, but about an ongoing committed relationship. Love and acceptance are the basis of such a union. A submissive should be first and foremost a trusted companion to the dominant. Obedience, which often stands firmly at the center of any spoken or written contract between a dominant and a submissive, grows out of the trust established by love.

**Honor.** While friendship and obedience develop between two people, honor is a matter of individual discretion and conscience. Honor is both a personal quality and a system of values according to which we make decisions. It is based on discernment, a realistic sense of order and fairness. There was a time when an honorable woman would not dream of "compromising herself" with pre- or extra-marital sex; for some people, this rule still holds true. A man of honor would not let a slanderous remark against himself or his family go unavenged. For the purposes of a submissive ethic, honor is an internal sense, one which allows the individual to make judgments about a given person, action, or situation. In the most general terms, "being honorable" is an old-fashioned way of saying that an individual has appropriate and consistent boundaries, that she is able to say, "This is acceptable; that, however, is not." It is vital for a submissive to be able to articulate her sense of honor, both in negotiation and in service.

"No, I refuse to speak badly of the Mistress in public." "No, I cannot serve you in any way that endangers my ability to earn a living or that compromises my physical and emotional safety." "No, I will not engage in behavior that my Owner has forbidden me, even though I know he'll never find out."

**Truthfulness**. A prerequisite to honor is truthfulness. Truthfulness is the ability to be honest with oneself and with others about one's feelings and motivations and to communicate these as accurately as possible. This quality includes the ability to say, "I don't know how I feel about that yet. Please give me some time to think about it," or "My feelings about that have changed. Here's where I stand now." If a submissive is not truthful, she cannot give informed consent, or more accurately, the dominant cannot be held responsible if, after complying with the submissive's expressed desires, the submissive complains. If she communicates a change in her feelings or perceptions – "I thought I'd like being put in a cage and ignored, but I found out I hated it" – that is one thing. That is being truthful. But complaints such as "You should have known not to call me a slut!" when no such boundary had been communicated are unacceptable. Any sentence that begins with "you should have known" indicates a lack of communication or of truthfulness.

**Humility**. Humility, like modesty, has an undeserved bad reputation. By humility I do not mean rampant self-deprecation or -hatred. I do mean a realistic perception of one's abilities and desires. This includes the ability to say to oneself and others, "I was wrong," or "I made a mistake," or "I misjudged my ability to do that for you." Likewise, a humble person will accept constructive criticism eagerly, finding in it the nugget of truth that is the key to self-betterment. Often our desire to please is so great that we undertake tasks for which we are not sufficiently prepared. There is nothing dishonorable about striving for a goal; what is dishonorable is the refusal to admit not being able to achieve that goal right now.

**Accomplishment.** Submissives, like knights, need to acquire special skills. A lady's maid will need extensive knowledge of make-up techniques and grooming, while a cook may want to attend a culinary school. The most famous courtly lover, Tristan, spoke many languages, played several instruments, was adept at hunting and dressing game, was an excellent fighter and statesman, and played a mean game of chess to boot. Self-betterment in one's chosen arts befits a submissive as well as it does a chivalrous knight.

**Courtesy.** We speak of the uncommon quality of common courtesy. Courtesy is, at base, a matter of respect. If we respect another person's time, personal space, and rights, then we will naturally act in a way that expresses that respect. If we respect their time, we will not arrive late to appointments. If we respect their personal space, we will not scatter our things around their home nor will we touch the person without invitation. We will allow them privacy. If we respect their rights, we will allow them to say "no" to us, to maintain their property, and to make decisions regarding their own health and welfare.

One must also be willing to extend such courtesy to oneself. We must, in all humility, respect our own needs for food, rest, privacy, recreation and the like. It is a discourtesy to others to be discourteous to oneself, in that denying our own human needs makes us all the more likely to disappoint our friend by being incapable or exhausted or otherwise unprepared for service.

**Fidelity**. Fidelity is a much-neglected virtue among submissives. As a group, submissives are infected with a scarcity mentality, which tells them that there are far too many bottoms and far too few tops. They feel this gives them permission to speak badly of a former partner in hopes of winning a new one, or to act as if a friend is only a friend as long as he does not stand in the way of a relationship with a desirable dominant. Yet, an honorable submissive can only gain from a refusal to compromise existing, valued friendships.

**Goodness (integrity)**. Integrity implies probity, a view of the self as a rounded and consistent whole. When a submissive strives to be "good," he is striving after integrity, the sense of security that comes from living in right relation to himself, the dominant, and the world.

The essence of goodness, of personal integrity, is compassion, a willingness to look into one's own heart and the hearts of others and be witness to human suffering. A compassionate submissive is one who will look beyond his own good and that of his master, to the greater goods of family and community A slave's acts of kindness reflect upon the dominant as well as upon the slave himself. The willingness to undertake an action simply because it is right marks a submissive as superior; indeed, he may be on the road to perfection.

## Support for submissives

As blissful as slavehood may be for those called to it, submissives run the risk of extreme isolation. It is vital that slaves maintain friendships outside of their dominant/submissive relationship, particularly with other slaves. Dominants should encourage such friendships, and any person who isolates a submissive from all other human contact is not dominant, but misguided. I encourage you to seek out BDSM organizations and publications that portray slavehood positively. Some of these organizations and publications are listed in the resource guide at the end of this book.

# Taxonomy of slavehood

The roles a submissive may play in the life of a dominant are as varied as that dominant's needs and her submissive's desires and skills. While many people envision slavehood according to the *Story of O* model, for a some submissives, genital sex is of secondary or even negligible importance. Such submissives find true satisfaction in the simple act of service and are therefore known as service-oriented submissives. What type of services can a submissive provide? Any and all!

**Houseslaves.** Imagine yourself in the home of a wealthy nineteenth-century British family. If you'vee seen reruns of "Upstairs, Downstairs" or "Brideshead Revisited" on PBS, you'll know exactly what I'm referring to – the place is crawling with servants.

When you arrived at your friends' home, you might first be met by a *footman* who would help you out of your carriage or, if you arrived on horseback, would see that your steed was taken safely to the stables. (The modern equivalent, of course, is the *chauffeur*.) At the door, the *butler* would greet you. The role of the butler – or in exceptionally wealthy households, the *steward* – is as the dignified head of the serving hordes. He – though in our day and age, a female butler is perfectly acceptable – sees to it that the household runs smoothly, that servants are generally neither seen nor heard, and that guests and family members are attended to. In general, he answers to no one but the master or mistress of the house. (You may have noticed that in novels butlers are often called by their last names; in the nineteenth century this was a mark of rank in service.) The butler often occupies a "middle" position – he is subordinate to his employers, but in charge of all the other servants. A dominant who has a number of slaves may elect a more experienced submissive to act as a butler or major domo in supervising the other slaves. The primary qualities of a good butler are loyalty and a strong sense of decorum. Submissives who feel called to the role of butler are often fastidious and detail-oriented and are comfortable juggling many tasks at once. They are the image of grace under pressure.

Both women and men may act very well as *maids*. (The special case of the transvestite or "sissy maid" will be discussed below.) Maids' duties include all aspects of household maintenance, such as cleaning, laundry shopping, and other errands. In some cases, an experienced maid, the *housekeeper*, may also supervise other servants. Some maids may serve in the kitchen, or a dominant may make use of a cook. If the dominant is so inclined, maids can be trained in special sorts of service, as, for example, tea service or serving at formal dinner parties. Older editions of etiquette manuals can provide a wealth of useful information for luncheon, tea, and dinner service for maids of more traditionally minded dominants.

Similar to the maid is the *houseboy*. This term is used for a servant of general usefulness who may do all that maids do in the home, but who is often employed at odd jobs – gardening, driving, carpentry and the like – in accordance with his training.

Related to the butler is the *valet*. Generally thought of in service to a dominant man, the valet acts as personal assistant in dressing and grooming. In certain periods, the valet was simply referred to as the master's "man." (Readers familiar with Dorothy Sayers's Lord Peter Wimsey mysteries will no doubt remember the inimitable Bunter.) The valet may also act in his master's stead, delivering messages, arranging schedules, and generally acting as a guy/gal friday.

The feminine (although not necessarily female!) counterpart to the valet is the *lady's maid*. Just as the valet is concerned with the master's wardrobe, so the lady's maid acts as hair stylist, costume consultant, and general companion to a dominant woman. A lady's maid is often on more intimate terms with her mistress, acting as confidante and counselor. In the nineteenth century, the lady's maid was given her mistress's old dresses and sewing scraps to keep or to sell.

Such are the traditional appointments for household servants.

**Sex slaves.** Many submissives' fantasies contain a distinctly erotic tone; indeed, most people engage in D/S play for the simple reason that it excites them. (And, in fact, no other reason is needed!) For some submissives, sexual servitude lies at the center of their eroto-emotional life. These submissives are best suited to be *sex slaves* or *sex toys*. In such arrangements, the sex slave exists for no other reason than the physical pleasure of the dominant. Often the slave's dress – or lack of it – will be designed to enhance her availability. While at the Chateau, O and her fellow slaves were required to wear elaborate dresses that exposed their breasts and genitals to all the company. When in the mundane world, René required O to go without panties, to seat herself with her bare rump flush against the seat, to keep her lips slightly parted to suggest openness to invasion, to wear blouses that allowed him access to her nipples, and so on. And just as O was initiated into anal sex by Sir Stephen, sex slaves should be trained in the specific sexual arts that please the dominant.

Of course, a slave of any type may also be used as a sex slave, if that is his desire and that of the dominant.

**Cross-dressers.** I have mentioned the *sissy maid* or panty slave. The subject of a whole sub-genre of erotic literature, the sissy maid is generally a man whose fantasy is to serve a lady while he is cross-dressed. The cross-dressing may be hidden (when the dominant orders the man to wear women's panties or stockings under his clothes) or transformational. In the latter case, the submissive strives to look as feminine as possible. He may wear a "gaff," a garment designed to hold the penis and testicles tucked under the body to give the illusion of a feminine shape under panties. Sissy maids are often employed for formal affairs or tea service. They may eroticize service in and of itself, or they may desire to be the object of the company's attention. Elaborate maid's costumes are available for these submissives, and the outfits range from the traditional short-skirted black and white dress to downright tarty red affairs.

**Slave without a master: Ronin.** What about a person who feels called to slavehood and yet has no master or who has lost his master? Such a submissive is sometimes called "ronin," the name for a "rogue" samurai warrior. Submissives can certainly undertake general training by themselves; many of the techniques I discuss here can be adapted to create an individual training program. If slavehood is indeed your calling, patience is in order. Cultivate yourself as if you were already serving your ideal master. There is no more effective way to attract him.

# Types of arrangements: the D/S relationship

Perhaps you have examined yourself closely, and know who you are and what you want. Perhaps you have even found the slave of your dreams. Now what? How do you make those dreams come true in our waking reality?

**Starting slow: the part-time D/S relationship.** I believe the phrase "casual dominant/submissive relationship" to be a contradiction in terms. I hold that effective and satisfying D/S relationships depend on genuine affection and intimacy between the partners, and affection and intimacy do not develop during a ten-minute negotiation at an S/M play party. Certainly dominant and submissive elements are an integral part of many S/M scenes, but the sort of service-oriented submission that I am discussing here does not lend itself to casual encounters.

This does not mean, however, that short-term or occasional D/S arrangements do not exist; in fact, they are quite common. The slave who cleans his Mistress's house once a month; the submissive carpenter who builds bondage equipment for her dominatrix friend in exchange for a session; two men who live 3,000 miles away from each other and negotiate a weekend-long contract once a year: all of these can be considered "casual," and yet clearly dominant/submissive, relationships. Indeed, many regular clients of professional dominants fall into this category. Over time, trust and a certain level of intimacy develop between client and dominant, and lifestyle dominants take the training of a sincere client very seriously. Acquaintances that begin as "casual" or occasional may well develop into long-term relationships.

**Telephone, computer, and postal training.** In our jet-set world, it is often impossible for a dominant and her slave to spend as much time together as they like. Even live-in slaves must sometimes be separated from their owners by business trips and family obligations. Luckily, it is not difficult to maintain contact across the miles.

Many professional dominants begin training potential clients by mail. The prospective client is expected to show proper respect and follow directions. The training may be as simple as returning a questionnaire or answering a letter, or it may require that the submissive assume a specific posture (kneeling, for example) while writing to the dominant, wear certain articles of clothing (panties, a cock ring), use special written forms of address, and send photos to prove that he has done his part. This sort of training can be adopted by other dominants as well. It is a wonderful option for individuals whose partners live at a distance or who travel a great deal.

A related form of training is by electronic mail. "Cyberslaves" have the advantage of instant contact with the dominant. There is some concern among Internet users that online exchanges may not be as private as we might hope. Anonymous fileservers do exist, and are one option to explore if privacy is an issue. The same techniques used in postal training are appropriate for e-mail, but the dominant should remember to leave the slave's hands – at least one of them! – unoccupied so that she can type.

There is an entire industry devoted to sexual encounters by phone, and people are often surprised to learn how many phone sex customers are looking for a dominant. Phone training demands a vivid imagination and some acting skill, but it has the added appeal of instant feedback – you can hear the passion and desire in a slave's voice, the demanding presence of the dominant in his speech.

BDSM "party lines" exist all over the country – check any mainstream pornographic magazine – although callers should take care not to give out too much information to strangers (home addresses, for example). Many professional dominants will do sessions by phone as well.

## "Please, Sir, may i have some more?": full-time relationships

**Total Slavehood: Fact or Fiction?** Many readers of BDSM erotica develop a curious tendency to confuse fiction and reality. Let me reiterate: *Story of O* is a work of fiction. That is, it is an artfully told lie that manages nonetheless to tell us something of the truth. But that truth is not literal. Certainly dominants pierce and brand their slaves; some may even own villas on the outskirts of Paris. But I'm afraid I must disappoint you: excruciatingly wealthy sadists with stables of nubile young women at their beck and call are not the norm. Such stories do express the depth of a submissive's desire, the passion a dominant feels at the willing submission of a loved one, and the often mysterious workings of the erotic imagination. To the extent that they portray these emotions, the stories are true.

This is not to say that full-time slaves and their masters do not exist. It has become a commonplace in introductory BDSM literature to pooh-pooh the concept of 24-hour-a-day, 7-day-a-week dominant/submissive relationships, and indeed, such correctives for the overactive imagination are necessary. Yet, to the extent that a slave arranges his life around his Master's and maintains constant awareness of his calling as a slave, I believe he embodies the ideal of the "total" slave. It is the ordering of one's life according to the principles of service that makes one a slave, not a collar or a contract or an afternoon workshop.

**Live-ins.** A "live-in" is, as the term suggests, a slave who lives with his or her dominant. In our imaginations, the live-in has become the archetypal slave, waiting patiently in a corner, naked and collared, always at his Master's beck and call. But how can relatively average people live like this?

There are three models for a live-in relationship: marital, dependent, and employee. It is instructive to look at the ways in which these models, as economic contracts, allow for a division of labor and responsibility between two parties.

In the marital or partner model, one person or both parties may work to earn an income, as is now the case in many domestic partnerships. In theory the dominant gets to say how the money is spent, although in practice, this task is often delegated to the submissive. The submissive is expected to run the household, provide for the comfort of the dominant on a day-to-day basis, and in return, can expect security and affection.

In the dependent model, the submissive is treated as a financial dependent, like a child. Here the submissive is supported by the dominant, or, if the submissive earns an income, he turns it over to the dominant. In most cases, the dominant saves or invests that money to create a trust fund for the submissive. In return, the submissive is expected to perform certain chores or tasks in the household. The submissive may be given an allowance, but he remains essentially dependent on the dominant.

The third model is the employer-employee model. In this case, the submissive lives rather like an au pair: he receives room, board and a modest sum of money in return for specific tasks, be they chauffeuring or shopping.

In practice, relationships run according to these models may look alike, but the assumptions that underlie them are very different. The marital model is first and foremost a partnership, and for that reason it is the most workable model for most people who are not independently wealthy. The dependent model presupposes that the dominant has or makes enough money to support two people, or has enough financial savvy to invest the submissive's money wisely. The au pair model is appropriate for dominants who work at home and need a personal secretary and for submissives with very specific, marketable talents. (My rule of thumb is, if the submissive would be paid for doing a task in the mundane world, she should receive equal recompense in some mutually agreeable form, be it legal tender, living space, or service trade.)

**Contracts**. Miss Abernathy is a great believer in contracts. There is a qualitative difference between saying "OK, you like canes, your safeword is 'mercy' and you hate gags. Got it!" and signing a piece of paper that specifies the rights and responsibilities of both parties. We live in a litigious culture, and contracts carry weight.

The basic purpose of a contract is to spell out, in as much detail as possible, the responsibilities of both parties, and the benefits they may expect.

The most notorious BDSM contracts are undoubtedly those that Leopold von Sacher-Masoch negotiated, on separate occasions, with his lovers, Fanny von Pistor and Wanda von Dunajew. Reprinted in Krafft-Ebing's famous work, *Psychopathia Sexualis,* they are two very different examples of contracts between a dominant and submissive. In the first, limited contract, Sacher-Masoch agreed "on his word of honor, to be Frau von Pistor's slave, to fulfill her every wish and command for a period of six months." For her part, Frau von Pistor agreed not to demand anything "dishonorable of SacherMasoch (i.e. that would make him dishonorable as a person or a citizen)"; to allow him time to work each day; to give him complete privacy in his correspondence and other writings, to punish him for his offenses according to her judgment; to wear fur as often as possible, "and especially when she is cruel." The contract also provided for re-negotiation and for long periods of interruption, at Frau von Pistor's discretion. As it stands, this contract can be adapted to fit the needs of modern dominants and submissives.

The contract between Sacher-Masoch and Wanda von Dunajew is somewhat lengthier and of a very different bent. In it, SacherMasoch gives up the pretense of bourgeois respectability that he had with Frau von Pistor, and signs over his body and soul to Wanda, giving her permission to make him a criminal and to "martyr him with all the torments imaginable, even to death."

I hope it will be clear from the preceding discussion that the second contract is a work of the erotic imagination, and it is hardly surprising that Krafft-Ebing saw in Leopold von Sacher-Masoch a man obsessed. It should also be clear that neither of these contracts would hold up in a court of law.

An example of a more modern and realistic contract can be found in *The Lesbian S/M Safety Manual* (ed. Pat Califia). Written by Diane Vera, the contract provides for the dominant's "full ownership and use of [the submissive's] body and mind" for a specified period of time. The contract enumerates the slave's responsibilities in general terms: obedience; renunciation of personal pleasure, except as permitted by the dominant; truthfulness; acceptance of criticism and punishment; effort to act in accordance with the dominant's wishes in all things. Most important, though, the submissive accepts the dominant's will "[w]ithin the limits of physical safety and [the submissive's] ability to earn a livelihood." In her notes on the contract, Vera states, "Except in authoritarian religious cults, I doubt that anyone can totally surrender his/her autonomy forever, though doing so temporarily can be an exciting and emotionally rewarding experience for some people."

Both Sacher-Masoch's and Vera's contracts are general; slave contracts can also be extraordinarily detailed. Clauses can and should include the following:

- safewords or some other signal for a "time-out"
- specific responsibilities of both parties, including financial ones
- circumstances under which the contract will become null and void
- any physical or psychological limitations of the parties
- who may and may not know about the contract, or read it

ecific rituals or formulas or titles that play a role in
lfillment of the contract

ussion of collars, tokens, and/or permanent marks

- punishments and rewards
- the beginning and ending dates of the contract

A preliminary contract should be negotiated for a short
period of time only – a weekend, or perhaps two weeks – after
which the contract should be re-negotiated and any changes
made. Some dominants prefer month-to-month contracts; others
opt for three- or six-month periods. People change more quickly
than contracts, so it is inadvisable to sign a contract for more than
a year at a time.

**Sample slave contract.** Obviously, the details of any contract
would depend on the circumstances and wishes of the signers.
The following is a rather extensive sample contract that may be
amended for more general use.

### Consensual Slave Contract

This document is intended to specify the
responsibilities of Jane Doe (hereafter "the
slave") and John Smith (hereafter "The Owner")
as part of a consensual arrangement between them.
This agreement is valid from midnight of January
1, 2007, through midnight of March 1, 2007. This
contract is a private agreement between the
parties and under no circumstances is it to be
read by anyone other than the undersigned.

This contract will become null and void if
any of the following circumstances should occur:

a)   either party becomes seriously ill, is
hospitalized, or dies, or

b)   either party is required to attend to
urgent family or business matters that will take

him or her away from home for more than fourteen
(14) days. In this event, the undersigned may
agree to put the contract on temporary "time out,"
and agree to negotiate for its reinstatement at
the earliest possible date.

I, Jane Doe, being of sound mind and body,
do hereby submit my will to that of the Owner,
John Smith. I wish to be his personal servant and
sex slave. I agree to fulfill, to the best of my
abilities, the following provisions.

1) The slave is to devote herself in mind and in
   body to the desires of the Oumer. She will
   obey him without question, knowing that he
   will never knowingly subject her to anything
   that will cause her physical or mental harm.

2) The Oumer agrees to attend to the physical,
   mental and emotional well-being ofthe slave.
   To enable him to do so, the slave will answer
   any question put to her as clearly and honestly
   as she is able.

3) The slave also agrees to make daily entries in
   a slave journal. Entries should be at least one
   page in length and are to be made in the approved
   written format, that is, without use of the first
   percon singular pronoun ("I" or "me") and any
   first person singular possessive pronouns ("my"
   or "mine"). In addition, all references to the
   slave are to be made in lower-case while all
   references to the Owner are to be capitalized.
   The journal is to be addressed to the Owner and
   will be read by him and him alone. Should this
   contract be dissolved, the slave will retain
   sole possession of the slave journal.

4) The slave will strive to maintain her health
   and vitality to better serve the Owner. She
   agrees to inform the Owner of any physical

discomfort, such as back or knee pain, that she may notice during the course of service. The Owner agrees to provide, at his expense, any medication necessary to treat conditions that result from service and to keep a supply of such medication at his home. The slave agrees to abstain from alcohol for 24 hours befrre any training session.

5) The slave agrees to maintain personal cleanliness in a manner suitable for service. She will remove all body hair on a regular basis and will rouge her nipples before each training session. When so orderered, she agrees to receive a cleansing enema from the Owner.

6) The slave agrees to wear whatever clothing the Owner may choose. This includes, but is not limited to, items of clothing (such as a corset) that the Owner may require her to wear under her street clothes.

7) The slave agrees to make her body available to the Owner whenever, wherever, and however he wishes. The Owner accepts full responsibility for the slave's safety and agrees not to require unprotected penis/vagina, penis/anus or penis/mouth sex from the slave.

8) The slave's training will include one formal S/M session per month. These sessions will always conclude with a formal caning. The slave acknowledges that these sessions may result in marks and agrees to inform the Owner if she expects to be in a circumstance (such as a doctor's visit or massage) where such marks might be a source ofunwanted attention.

9) The slave acknowledges that the safeowrd is "Mercy." If she calls "Mercy," the Owner will immediately cease whatever activity is

in progress. The slave will then b
sufficient opportunity to voice her
or make requests. The Owner will then, to the
best of his ability and in full consideration
of the slave's well-being, decide whether to
proceed with the activity.

10) The Owner will furnish all tools and implements
of correction as well as safer sex supplies.
The single exception to this clause is that
the slave will be expected to provide the Owner
with a cane, to be used on her only at the
beginning of the first formal S/M session. The
slave will be expected to clean and maintain
all tools, including this cane.

11) In accordance with the slave's previously
stated limits, the Owner agrees not to use
language that calls into question the slave's
intelligence, nor will he use language,
gestures, or scenarios that put the slave in
the role of an animal.

12) Should she displease the Owner, the slave
agrees to submit to whatever punishment the
Owner may deem necessary. In accordance with
the slave's previously stated limits, the
Owner agrees not to use a belt as an implement
of correction. Punishments will be for the
betterment of the slave only and will not be
undertaken in anger.

13) The Owner agrees to furnish the slave with a
token which symbolizes his complete possession
of the slave. This token will be suitable to
wear in all circumstances, and the slave is
expected to wear it at all times.

14) In addition to the token, the Owner will
provide a collar which the slave is to wear
while serving in the Owner's home and while at

leather community events. The collar remains the property of the Owner and is a symbol of his responsibilities toward the slave.

15) The slave is to address the Owner as "Sir" or "Sir John" unless otherwise directed. The slave will speak to the Owner with respect. This respect should extend to speaking of the Owner as well.

16) The slave agrees to perform, to the best of her ability, whatever household tasks the Owner requires of her. These will routinely include, but are not limited to, the following: washing, drying, ironing, folding and putting away the laundry; sweeping and/or vacuuming the floors; preparing three dinners and one brunch per week.

17) While in the Owner's home, the slave must ask permission before using any furniture, using the toilet, or eating with utensils.

18) The slave will be expected to accompany the Owner to one leather community social event each month. She agrees to "attend" the Owner at these events and renounces the right to move freely while doing so.

signed, this day_____ 20_____

Jane Doe, slave_____

John Smith, Owner_____

# Ending an association: the importance of prenuptials

I believe that any contract between a dominant and a submissive – and any negotiation, for that matter – should include an explicit agreement about what will happen should the association not work out. I call these agreements "pre-nuptials." We all know about the "honeymoon" period when new lovers float about, four feet off the ground. Once they come back to earth, the view can be very different.

If the dominant is contracting for a live-in slave, the pre-nuptial clause(s) should include provisions ensuring the material and emotional care of the slave should the dominant dissolve the contract.

Certainly any income that the dominant has controlled or saved for the slave should be returned immediately, with interest. Any personal items that belonged to the slave before the contract should also be returned. I also suggest that the slave be given the option of retaining any written work produced at the dominant's command, such as journals or essays, or at least copies of these.

But will the dominant be responsible for any or all of the shve's moving costs, which can include sizable security deposits and rental fees? What about household items or toys bought during the contract with both parties' money? Is it the slave's blender because she used it more, or the dominant's because he paid for it with his credit card? When a relationship is ending, the last thing anyone wants is more grief. Spell it out. I strongly suggest consulting an attorney for advice on pre-nuptial clauses before signing a live-in contract. You can always pretend you're actually getting married or establishing a domestic partnership, if discretion is an issue. At very least, look at some of the excellent do-it-yourself law books available from Nolo Press that show sample contracts and pre-nuptial agreements. Many books written for newlyweds include sections on finances and prenuptials. A contract between a dominant and a submissive is a commitment of no less importance or complexity than any other relationship, whether the State acknowledges it or not. Often marriage is the only comparable situation, and dominants and submissives would do well to learn where they can.

In more formal, traditional dominant/submissive relationships, the dominant will take the lead, and that includes the prerogative of ending the relationship. I do not wish to imply that a slave has no right to end a relationship or that they are a "bad" slave for doing so, simply that the dynamics of such relationships often leave more room for the dominant to initiate change. One well-known dominant woman of my acquaintance feels strongly that it is not just her prerogative, but her responsibility, to end a relationship that may be damaging to the submissive's self-esteem or general well-being, whether or not the submissive believes that to be the case. Whiie this attitude may at first glance seem arrogant, it in fact speaks of a commitment to care for the submissive, and an understanding of the pitfalls of submission. This is not the same thing as Wanda Syndrome, and this dominant is hardly giving herself permission to throw a slave out on her ear. Rather, she takes responsibility for the slave's well-being.

A word to slaves: I have had the misfortune to know a number of submissives who seem to believe that the dissolution of a contract gives them license to behave badly. You will have realized by now that I view slavehood as a noble vocation, and I expect a slave to act no less honorably than a dominant in the event that a relationship ends.

Here are a few simple guidelines, which I believe constitute the basis for good manners and a good reputation (and, should it not be clear from the discussion above, let me say that these principles apply no less to dominants than to submissives):

- Return all of the dominant's property to her. This may include, but is not limited to, collars; tokens of ownership not explicitly given to the slave (name tags or other jewelry); house and car keys; any legal documents (although the slave should certainly retain a copy of the contract itself); credit cards or checks issued in the dominant's name, any items borrowed from the dominant, such as clothing, or borrowed in the dominant's name, such as rented video tapes, library books, and the like. Needless to say, any fees incurred due to the submissive's neglect to return borrowed items should be promptly paid by the submissive.

- Refrain from denigrating the dominant to mutual friends or in public. Unless you feel strongly that the dominant is a genuine menace to public safety – in which case you might as well speak to the police as to your friends – spreading malicious gossip in the community will only damage your own reputation. I do not wish to imply that a slave should not seek solace from his friends, and it is likely that some of these friends will also be acquainted with the dominant. (Here is an important reason for a submissive to cultivate friendships outside the BDSM community and outside his D/S relationship.) Still, it is unfair to expect mutual friends to take your side, or to take sides at all. Be as respectful of the dominant's privacy as you would expect him to be of yours.

- Give yourself sufficient time to heal from any emotional wounds you may have suffered in the relationship. Do not jump into another D/S relationship too quickly. It will typically take anywhere from one year to three for a person to work through the pain of a failed relationship. Resist the urge to fall at the feet of the next dominant who waves a collar in your direction. By all means, go out, socialize, play if you will, but if you attempt another relationship too quickly, you are likely to deliver damaged goods to the new dominant and doing yourself a great disservice.

# In Conclusion

While it takes a great deal of forethought, hard work, and dedication to create and maintain a successful D/S arrangement, the benefits to both dominant and submissive are immeasurable. In conclusion, I would like to share with you, gentle reader, the story of a very happy slave.

We will call him G. At this writing, he lives in a major American city, across the street from his Master, a well-known figure in the local leather community. The Master is in a committed relationship with another young man, his "boy." G. shows incredible devotion to his Master. He has arranged his life so that he may be at his Master's disposal at any time of day or night. This has meant taking an apartment close to his Master's home and finding a job that would allow him to wear his collar – a solid length of chain with a heavy padlock – to work.

It is essential to G's submission that he be ever and always his Master's. I have seen him walking down the street. He is a tall man and carries himself with such reserved dignity that strangers passing him stop and follow him with questioning eyes as he proceeds down the block. He treats friend and stranger alike with respect and grace.

It is not just that he knows that any flaw in his deportment will be reported to his Master by mutual friends, of whom they have a great many in the city. He simply wants nothing more than to be a tribute to his Master at all times. And is that not the root of submissive desire?

# Training With Miss Abernathy

a workbook for erotic slaves and their owners

# Introduction

Allow me to be the first to welcome you to Miss Abernathy's Academy. Whether you are an old friend or are investigating your interest in consensual dominance and submission for the first time, I hope you will find something of value between the covers of this modest volume.

Please take a moment to read this introduction before proceeding, as it will give you the necessary background to make the most of your time with us.

## For whom is this book intended?

I have designed this program so that it can be used equally well by several different groups of people. First, trainers of erotic slaves can use the book as the basis for a comprehensive program lasting from three to twelve months or longer. Those who already own a slave but are looking for some new ideas or want to direct the slave to a new level of expertise or specialization will also find the book of use. Finally, I envision the possibility that submissives who are not currently in service, but would like to be, will use this book as a self-directed training program, following their own talents and interests. Since there seem to be relatively few experienced trainers, and many willing and able submissives, I have generally addressed the text directly to the submissive.

# What is slave training?

For our purposes here, slave training is to be understood as the process by which a person gains the necessary skills and attitudes to willingly serve another person. During this process, the trainee may be properly called a submissive, by which we mean a person who knowingly and willingly gives control of certain parts of his or her life over to another person or persons; we may also refer to such a person as a slave-in-training. A submissive nature may be an inborn quality or a set of learned behaviors – opinions vary on this point – but observation shows that submissives are at their happiest and most fulfilled when allowed to express their submissive desires. One way of expressing submission is through specific acts of service performed for the benefit or pleasure of a dominant. In performing these acts of devotion for another, submissives also serve their own deepest desires and highest purpose. In short, service is their vocation. Therefore, we sometimes refer to them as "service-oriented submissives."

As we shall see, this service may take many forms, from simple acts of obedience to complex roles involving considerable intelligence, skill, and dedication. As you work through this program, you will learn about the types of service for which you are best suited and which you most enjoy. Dominants, for their part, derive deep satisfaction from ordering another's life, and nothing brings them more pleasure than seeing a task performed with skill, love, and devotion. Whether the job is as simple as washing the dishes and making the bed or as complex as organizing a home office or cooking a gourmet meal, the thrill the dominant experiences is directly proportional to the submissive's effort and dedication.

Consequently, you will find that this program focuses at least as much on developing the correct attitudes as it does on attaining certain skills. No matter how technically correct the execution of a task may be, without the inner sense of earnest dedication a submissive brings to the work, the result is worthless.

# Why this book?

Some readers may already be familiar with my first book, *Miss Abernathy's Concise Slave Training Manual.* In it, I set out my personal theories of erotic slave training. As the title implies, the *Manual* was designed as a guide for trainers. It focused on ethics and etiquette as much as on concrete suggestions for training activities, as I deem these considerations of equal importance. In short, the Manual was the theory; this book is the practice.

Dominant/submissive (D/S) culture is, on the whole, under-represented in the field of BDSM* non-fiction *[although this situation has changed for the better since the publication of this book; see Bibliography – Ed.].* In addition, most of the available material focuses on a specific gender or sexual orientation; this book, in contrast, is pansexual in its range.

Miss Abernathy firmly believes that the time has come for us to view slavehood as a vocation that requires not just desire, but dedication. I hope that, by giving the wider BDSM community more information about the intricacies of slave training and psychology, I can help increase the respect of this community for submissives and their trainers.

---

*BDSM is a catch-all acronym for the related practice of "bondage and discipline" (B/D), "dominance and submission" (D/S) and sadomasochism (S/M).*

# How to use this book

As I have already suggested, this program can be used by trainers, owners, and unaffiliated submissives alike. I strongly encourage all readers to work through the "Preliminaries" section (trainers will find the material for a slave interview here) and at very least review the information presented in the "Basic Training" section. The "Household Management" section will be of use to those beginning domestic service, but as it is also a prerequisite for the most of the material presented in "Area Studies," it has been given under a separate heading.

After completing the first three sections, the slave-in-training may wish to proceed to the more specialized Area Studies that reflect his or her interests and talents as well as the dominant's service needs. Despite a higher degree of specialization at this point in the training process, readers will find some overlaps. Related lessons have been cross-referenced for your convenience.

Even if you have your heart set on being a sex slave or a lady's maid, don't neglect your training in other areas. Diversified training will only increase your value to the dominant, and you may discover with pleasure a new area of interest or talent.

The course of training is designed to take approximately one week per lesson, although of course it is acceptable to move more slowly. I must caution beginners (particularly those working without the benefit of a trainer) from moving much more quickly, as it is important to let your emotions and body catch up with your mind. If you encounter a difficulty, it is always appropriate to slow down or even to set the work aside for a time until you feel better able to take it up again. Remember that slave training in its most intense form involves nothing less than a remaking of one's life priorities. It is not a process that can be rushed.

# Who is Miss Abernathy?

Miss Abernathy notes with gratitude the interest expressed in certain quarters about her person. Let it be known, then, that Miss Abernathy is a dominant persona of an experienced BDSM practitioner living in the San Francisco Bay Area. *[See Editor's Notes for update – Ed.]* My education and travels have left their mark on me in the form of an insatiable curiosity about human nature, while my background in teaching has given me a taste for the joys of helping others expand their capacities. Within the D/S world, I have had the privilege to train under several notable dominants, in whose debt I shall forever stand. Since that time, I have had the equal privilege of training a number of talented and dedicated submissives. In addition, the local BDSM community has afforded me an unparalleled opportunity to observe and participate in an ever-changing discussion of BDSM theory and practice. I have also been in the unusual position to observe both the men's and women's leather communities, as well as the pansexual and transgender ones.

I hope that my experience in and love of these erotic arts will only serve to benefit you, gentle reader, as you undertake this exciting adventure.

Yours most truly,

*Christina Abernathy (Miss)*

# Preliminaries

In these first weeks, you will be exploring your ideas about submission, learning about the different kinds of slaves, examining your strengths and weaknesses, assessing the risks in undertaking this training, and looking at your expectations of the coming weeks. If you are working with a trainer, you will be asked to share your thoughts and feelings about slavehood in a verbal slave interview*. The written exercises in this section should help you clarify your own ideas; they may also form part of the interview process itself. If you are studying independently, please give yourself sufficient time to complete the exercises. Also, you may wish to consult the opening pages of *Miss Abernathy's Concise Slave Training Manual* (hereafter simply the Manual) if you have any questions about terminology or the concept of consent in D/S relationships.

# Lesson 1. What is a slave?

In this first lesson, you will be exploring your ideas about slavehood.

---

* *Please do not allow doubts about your literary talents, spelling skills, or penmanship to deter you from completing the written exercises. Their value lies chiefly in their use as a tool for uncovering your thoughts, emotions, and insights, none of which need to be spelled correctly to be valid.*

*Exercise.* Take three slow, deep breaths and clear your mind. Jot down twenty words, phrases, images, or associations that come to mind when you hear the word "slave." Give yourself no more than two minutes to complete this exercise. Do not think; write.*

Now, look at your list. Surprised? Even if you have very positive ideas about D/S and your submissive feelings, you may find that your subconscious holds some unpleasant associations with the concept. It is not unusual for the mind to toss up images of brutality, nonconsensual violence, and painful socio-historical models. These images are the source of an uneasiness that you may feel about D/S.

You are not sick or perverted. Why? Because you have control over your choices. You rule your own desires, and one of the options you have is to turn control of those desires over to another person. You have the inalienable right to consent. (You also have the equally inalienable right not to.)

*Activity:* On an index card or other piece of paper, write an affirmation of your right to consent. If you are not familiar or comfortable with the process of composing affirmations, you can use one of these:
- I have the unalienable right to consent.
- I control my own destiny.
- I choose to live a life of right action in service.

Place this sign someplace where you'll see it several times a day, such as a desk drawer, or your bathroom mirror, or the refrigerator door.

You may find affirmations "hokey" or 'too New Age." You are allowed to find them silly. You are also allowed to give them a try, with no obligations.

**Suggested Reading\*:** *Sacred Moments: Daily Meditations on the Virtues* **by Linda Kavelin Popov.**

# Lesson 2. What kind of a slave am I?

The best slaves are versatile people. They are able to rise to the challenge of a new task with grace. Still, most slaves – like other people – possess certain talents that they do well to cultivate. Likewise, they may have a burning interest in one aspect or another of slavehood, while other facets leave them cold. While Miss Abernathy would like to encourage her readers not to limit themselves too early, it may be helpful for you to look at your own ideas and preferences regarding slavehood.

---

*Exercise:* Imagine you are a live-in slave, serving your ideal dominant. What would your life be like? Choose the answer that most closely fits your dream.

1. At 6 a.m. I am suddenly awakened by...
   a. Mistress's bell.
   b. Mistress's foot.
   c. the alarm clock.
   d. the wake-up call.
2. It's time to get dressed. I put on...
   a. my uniform.
   b. nothing.
   c. an apron.
   d. a suit.

---

\* *As part of this training program, I suggest books and other resources that I believe to be of use to slaves-in-training. Do not feel compelled to purchase all or even most of them: you will find them just as easily at your local public library. If you find them of more enduring value, then by all means, obtain a copy for your personal collection. A Bibliography can be found in the back of this book.*

3. It's a busy day. I spend the morning...

    a.       mending Master's riding breeches.

    b.       pleasuring Master.

    c.       cleaning the hall closet.

    d.       attending Master as he tours the city.

4. Time for lunch! I eat...

    a.       in the sitting room.

    b.       off Mistress's boot.

    c.       whenever I get a minute.

    d.       in a nice little café Mistress likes.

5. The best thing about being a slave is...

    a.       being close to Master.

    b.       the sex.

    c.       feeling useful.

    d.       experiencing new things.

6. My strong point is...

    a.       my knowledge of fashion.

    b.       my sex appeal.

    c.       my organizational skills.

    d.       my people skills.

7. The hardest part of being a slave is...

    a.       finding time to keep myself looking good.

    b.       getting my intellectual needs met.

    c.       the details, all the little details.

    d.       being on show all the time.

8. After dinner...

    a.       Master reads the paper while I polish his shoes.

    b.       we retire to the boudoir.

    c.       I do the dishes.

    d.       we're off to the theater with the Billings-Joneses.

9. Time for bed. I must...
    a.      lay out Mistress's outfit for tomorrow.
    b.      make myself available in case Mistress wants a massage.
    c.      review tomorrow's menu.
    d.      get some sleep after pleasuring Mistress. I've got to look my best.

10. I dream about...
    a.      being allowed to accompany Master on a drive.
    b.      the day Master lets me masturbate for him.
    c.      a nice long bubble bath and an intimate dinner out with Master.
    d.      just staying home one weekend and relaxing.

---

Now, count the number of times you answered (a), (b), (c), or (d). Does any one letter predominate? If so, you may have a natural specialty, as explained below. If your answers fall consistently into two categories, you may be attracted to two related or complementary roles. If your answers are varied, you may be best suited for more general service, or you may still discover another specialty not covered here. Finally, if you notice that you never chose a specific letter, you may feel less enthusiastic about a particular type of service. It is still to your benefit to learn something about that specialty so that your training will be well-rounded.

If you chose mostly (a) answers, you may be a good body servant (lady's maid or valet). You value intimacy with the dominant above all else. You are aware of the importance of your physical appearance, and you like to help others look their best. You like personal attention from the dominant and are proud of any trust s/he places in you. You are most comfortable serving at home, although you enjoy it when guests come to visit because it gives you a chance to display your pretty manners. If you also had a number of (b) answers, you may also enjoy sexual service or Victorian scenarios. If you answered (c) to several questions, you might be a good all-around housekeeper, especially in a small home. If you answered (d) to some questions, you might like to travel with the dominant as a personal secretary or escort.

If you chose mostly (b) answers, you are probably most interested in being a sex slave. You are a highly sexual person with considerable stamina, and you pride yourself on your sexual technique. While most slaves enjoy some sexual attention, the erotic side of slavehood is your main focus. You may be willing to perform some domestic service tasks, especially if you are rewarded with the privilege of pleasuring the dominant. If you had some (a) answers, you might consider learning about massage or makeup application to complement your sexual skills. If you had some (c) answers, you may want to include more household management as part of your training. If you had a number of (d) answers, you may want to focus on your conversation skills to become an escort.

If you chose mostly (c) answers, you are best suited to be a housekeeper and/or cook. You are very organized and have considerable household management skills. You are comfortable dealing with visitors and shopping for the household's needs, but you're just as happy behind the scenes. You don't need very much personal attention and are a self-starter. You derive the greatest satisfaction from attending to the dominant's needs in a quiet, unobtrusive way. If you had some (a) answers, you may want to be closer to the dominant and help with some personal care. If you had some (b) answers, you may fantasize about being used sexually while in the middle of some other task. If you had some (d) answers, you may also have the makings of an excellent personal secretary.

If you chose mostly (d) answers, you want to be an escort. You have an attractive personality and excellent communication skills. You enjoy meeting new people and serving in public. You don't mind if some people think you're the dominant's lover; the two of you know the truth about your relationship. Besides, you're very discreet. If you also had some (a) answers, you may enjoy a more formal role, at least at home or in private. A few (b) answers indicate that you would enjoy attending the dominant at BDSM functions and joining in the fun yourself. If you have some (c) answers, you'd be an excellent butler or personal secretary.

## Lesson 3. Assessing strengths and weaknesses

When you serve another, you are making a gift of yourself to that person. Your value as a slave – beyond the basic intrinsic value of your humanity – relates directly to the skills and attitudes you bring to the relationship.

For a dominant, much of the joy in owning a slave is in the training, so do not think that you will be rejected if you don't know everything right at the start. At its best, service is a lifelong vocation, and you will never stop learning.

Every journey begins somewhere. In this lesson, you'll be looking at the skills you already have – and those you don't – as a way of planning your itinerary for the weeks to come.

*Exercise:* List five things you do very well: cook, type, repair cars, give massages, listen, perform oral sex on men...

List five things you don't know how to do, but would like to learn: speak French, decorate cakes, do your own taxes, skydive...

List five things you are embarrassed about not being able to do well: draw, eat with chopsticks, enjoy foreign films...

Ust five things you love to do but would never admit to in public: watch professional wrestling, masturbate, eat pork rinds...

*Activity*: In the next week, choose one of the items from the second list – things you'd like to learn – and research how you might begin to learn it. Is there a class you could take? A book you could read? A friend you could ask for help? Begin the journey this week.

# Lesson 4. Responsibilities of a slave-in-training

One of the most important responsibilities of a slave-in-training is communication. You will be required not only to communicate about everyday things and to report on your activities, but you will also be expected to speak frankly about your inner life.

If you haven't spent much time thinking about your own life's path, you may find it uncomfortable to "confess" your dreams and feelings to another person. In fact, many people cannot, without prompting, name the emotions that they are experiencing at any given moment. It is vital that a slave develop a self-reflective impulse: the habit of examining him- or herself on a regular basis so as to be able to describe accurately and unselfconsciously his or her own state of mind.

The following exercise is designed to help you make the first steps in developing this healthful habit. It is important to keep your hand moving across the page as you answer these questions. Write whatever first comes to mind; your answers are not carved in stone, but are the fluid bubblings of your unconscious mind. You may wish to analyze your answers later, but for now, simply write.

*Exercise:* Complete the following sentences.

I imagine myself as a slave being able to...

As a slave, I wouldn't be allowed to...

The idea that those things would be forbidden makes me feel...

Just once in my life, I'd like to...

I definitely would not want to...

In my sexiest private fantasy, I...

I have a secret fetish for...

Being in a collar would make me feel...

If I were forbidden to have an orgasm for a whole week, I'd...

When I masturbate, I often think about...

I'd like to learn how to...

Serving my Master or Mistress in public would make me feel...

My most erotic memory is...

I first learned about erotic slavehood when...

My favorite book is...

My favorite movie is...

In my free time, I most often...

The thing I find most attractive in other people is...

My highest priority in life is...

Sometimes I doubt I'll ever be able to...

I think most of my romantic involvements have been...

In the past, I was ashamed of...

I feel I've come to terms with...

If there's one negative emotion I can't handle, it's...

When a person raises their voice to me, I...

The three things I associate with silence are...

If pressed, I'd identify myself as...
The biggest influence on my erotic life has been...
I'd describe my spiritual life as...
I believe strongly that..
I'd fight for my right to...
I've only ever wanted to...

**Suggested Reading:** If you find it difficult to name your feelings, you may find *The Book of Qualities* by J. Ruth Gendler enlightening.

# Lesson 5. Assessing risk: your relationships, work, and health

All changes involve risk. Risk-taking is an integral part of growth and learning. As you work on the following exercise, you will assess the risks you may take by entering into a slave training program.

Often when we start to follow our dreams, we experience conflict with people around us. This conflict can be the result of envy, fear, confusion, or a simple lack of information. In order to make an informed decision – that is, to give your consent to beginning a training program – you need to look carefully at your relationships and the effect that your new work may have on them. This exercise may seem daunting, especially if your friends are not knowledgeable about D/S or have expressed concerns about your involvement with it. By facing obstacles head-on, you stand the best chance of overcoming them.

The same holds true for your work life and your health. Training as a slave will present you with new and exciting challenges. It is important for you to take a careful look at your limitations, so that you can communicate them to your trainer. There is no shame in having limits, only in disregarding them.

## Relationships

*Exercise:* Rate your responses to the following statements. Use a scale of 1-10 where 1 means "never" or "absolutely not" and 10 means "always" or "most definitely."

- I am most comfortable when in a monogamous relationship.
- I enjoy feeling helpless or "out of control" sometimes.
- I am attracted to members of my own gender.*
- I am uncomfortable if I don't know what my partner is thinking.
- My family knows about my interest in D/S and they're all right with it.**
- My friends know about my interest in D/S and they're supportive of my choices.
- If my neighbors found out about my interest in D/S, it wouldn't bother them in the least.
- My therapist is comfortable discussing my interest in D/S and seems to know something about consensual BDSM.***

---

* *If your response to this statement was, "I'd answer if I knew what gender I was, then you may enjoy Kate Bornstein's* My Gender Workbook.

** *While Miss Abernathy acknowledges that opinions on child-rearing vary greatly, she feels compelled to express her strong conviction that it is inappropriate – and potentially harmful – to involve children in adult sexual relationships. It is inappropriate to divulge the details of your private life to any children in your care. It is also important to assess how any responsibilities you might take on as a slave-in-training would affect your ability to care for children, and make your decisions accordingly.*

*** *For a list of therapists and other professionals who are knowledgeable about BDSM, visit www.ncsfreedom.org/kap/index.htm.*

## Work

*Exercise:* Describe your current job (or other sources of income). In what ways do you imagine slavehood might affect your work? If your employer or co-workers found out about your interest in D/S, what would be the most likely outcome?

If you quit your job today, where would you stand financially?

**Suggested Reading: Much BDSM erotica might lead you to believe that only those of independent means can be dominants and that all submissives should be ready to drop their careers, living spaces, and friends at a moment's notice in order to serve. As a reality check, I suggest you read the opening chapters of two well-known D/S classics and compare how the authors handle the issue of money. First read John Preston's *Mr. Benson*, and then turn to *The Slave* by Laura Antoniou. Which book seems more realistic to you?**

## Health

*Activity:* Ask your doctor for a copy of your medical history for your own files. Make a list of all the medications (including over-the-counter drugs, medicinal herbs, vitamins, and nutritional supplements) that you use. Date the list, and add this to your medical history file. Be sure to update the list as needed.

*Activity:* If you have not had a thorough general physical for more than three years, schedule an appointment with your doctor for one. This is especially important if you have any unusual health problems.

---

*Exercise:* Answer the following questions in detail and be scrupulously honest. A positive answer to any of these questions does not disqualify someone for service. In fact, those who have weathered adversity are often stronger and enjoy greater self-knowledge than their "more fortunate" peers, making them especially well-prepared for training. It is vital, in any case, that your trainer have this information to help maintain your personal safety. If you are working without a trainer, consider the implications of your answers. Would a lifestyle change or professional assistance make it easier for you to serve?

- Do you have any allergies?
- Do you have any dietary restrictions? Are you vegetarian or vegan?
- Do you have any chronic illnesses or injuries that trouble you? What sort of treatment do you use?
- Do you wear eyeglasses or contact lens? A hearing aid?
- Do you use any drugs (including alcohol or tobacco) recreationally? What and how often?
- Are you currently struggling with an addiction?
- Are you aware of any body image issues that trouble you?
- Are you clean and/or sober? For how long?

- Are you in recovery from an addiction other than alcohol or drugs? For how long?
- Did you suffer any abuse (physical, verbal, psychological, sexual, spiritual...) as a child?
- Have you suffered such abuse as an adult?
- How have you learned to heal these wounds?
- If you have a history of abuse, can you identify any "triggers" (words, sounds, objects, situations) that might cause you trauma now?
- Do you have any history of abusing others? If so, what steps have you taken to change this pattern?

*Suggested Reading: The Body Image Workbook*, by Thomas F Cash.; *Esteem Comes in All Sizes*, by Carol A. Johnson.

*Resources:* Many major cities now have recovery groups for BDSM practitioners. Call your local AA or NA Central Office for details.

# Lesson 6. Expectations: the training contract

The purpose of a training contract is to spell out, in detail, the respective responsibilities of the trainer and the trainee. It may be useful for you to think of the training contract in terms of an "at-will" employment agreement. Such an agreement states that both employer and employee reserve the right to cancel the agreement at will and explains the process for doing so. (This generally includes the requirement that either party give written notice the other in the event that the agreement is to be dissolved.) Further, it specifies the starting date of employment, a job description, salary and any benefits that the employer will provide, such as health insurance, transit costs, or uniforms.

If you are working with a trainer, no doubt he or she will have a standard contract for you to examine. If you believe that you will be unable to fulfill any clause of the contract or do not wish to do so, it is your right – indeed, your obligation – to ask for further negotiation until you can reach a mutually agreeable compromise.

All training contracts should include the following:

- the starting date and ending dates of the contract;
- the specific responsibilities of both parties, including financial ones;
- safewords or some other signal for a "time-out";
- physical and psychological limitations of the parties;
- a discussion of punishment (what forms it may take, when it will be used…);
- any specific rituals or formulas or titles that play a role in the fulfillment of the contract;
- circumstances under which the contract will become null and void;
- the goal of the contract. (This may be as simple as "the training of a slave to our mutual satisfaction" or a list of skills to be acquired; it may also include a philosophical statement on the nature of slavehood as the trainer understands it.)

How can a slave working independently draw up a contract? Since a training contract is an agreement between two (or more) people, clearly an individual cannot be subject to one. Miss Abernathy instead suggests that such a submissive write a Statement of Purpose in which he or she makes a personal commitment to work through the training program. Since you are essentially both trainer and trainee, be sure to specify the responsibilities you have toward yourself: excellent self-care, sufficient food, sleep, exercise, and recreation, and most of all, compassion.

# Basic Training

## Lesson 7. Obedience I: first steps toward mindfulness

If you were to ask one hundred submissives for a definition of "obedience," ninety-five of them would tell you that means doing as you're told or following orders. In the strict sense, they would be correct.

But what if you received the following order: "Tell me what you are feeling right now!" Would you be able to answer clearly and accurately?

And what about the situations in which no verbal command is issued? Perhaps you are faced with a difficult choice and the dominant is not present to guide you. How can you act in the spirit of obedience if the "letter of the law" is missing?

---

*Exercise:* After you finish reading the instructions for this exercise, but without looking around you first, close your eyes. Now name three things in the room that are behind you, to your right, to your left, and in front of you.

---

This exercise will have given you some insight into your skills of observation. The next time you are in an unfamiliar environment, try the exercise again. Does being in a new place change your observations?

Now you will learn a technique to help you observe not only your physical surroundings, but also yourself.

---

*Activity:* Sit comfortably with your spine straight. You may choose to sit in a chair or cross-legged on the floor, as long as you can maintain the position for at least twenty minutes. Do not lie down, as this posture encourages drowsiness.

Now, close your eyes, and draw your attention to your breath. Observe how the breath enters your nostrils as you inhale and exits as you exhale. Focus your awareness on the point where the breath enters and exits. If thoughts or feelings surface – and they will – simply return your attention to your breath. Do not judge or follow your thoughts; simply return to the breath. Count ten full breaths (in and out). When you are finished, slowly become aware of your surroundings. When you are ready, open your eyes.

---

The purpose of this meditation is to help you quiet your mind and to be able to observe the flow of thoughts that arise as you do so. The content of the thoughts is irrelevant. What is important is the insight that the mind is in constant motion, and that it is very difficult to stop or control that motion. We also observe that as thoughts arise, so also do they pass.

Try this meditation every day for at least one week; you may choose to make it a regular part of your training. At first you may only be able to count a single breath before thoughts and feelings come crowding in. This is normal. If you persist – just letting the thoughts pass by like boats on a stream – you will be able to distance yourself from your thoughts and feelings. This distance will allow you the space to name and describe your thoughts and feelings without getting caught up in them.

> *Suggested Reading:* **Any book or tape by Fr. Thomas Keating or Thich Nhat Hanh. You need not be Catholic or Buddhist to appreciate the universality of the meditation techniques they teach.**

Along with awareness of your inner workings, it is important to cultivate awareness of your physical self. Most submissives find it very difficult to hold their bodies still for any length of time, but this is a vital skill for a slave.

---

*Activity:* For this activity, you will need a watch with an unobtrusive alarm function, ideally one that emits a single beep. (You can also use a small alarm clock or timer, as long as the alarm isn't too loud and doesn't beep continuously until you turn it off.) You will be carrying this alarm with you through your day.

Set the alarm to sound at 11 minutes past the hour. When the alarm sounds, bring your attention to your physical posture: Where are your hands? Are your legs crossed? Is your back straight? Your jaw tense? Do you feel any pain in your body? Are you moving any part of your body (jiggling your leg, chewing on a pencil)? When you've assessed your physical state, you may want to take a moment to relax any tension that you've discovered. Now, reset the alarm for the next hour.

---

*Activity:* Do you remember the card game Memory? In it, a special deck of cards (or two complete standard decks) are dealt out face down in even rows, The first player turns over two cards. If they match, the player removes them from the table and takes another turn. If they do not match, the player turns them back over and the other player takes a turn. Whoever makes the most matches, wins.

Try this game alone or with a friend. It will help you to develop better observation skills.

# Lesson 8. Obedience II: awareness of others

The slave-in-training has to strike a careful balance between self-observation and awareness of others. A slave is often called upon to respond to requests indicated by the slightest hand gesture, the half-smile, the raised eyebrow.

If you live in a crowded city or in an active home, you may have learned to "tune out" the hustle and bustle that surrounds you. In this lesson, you will learn to tune back in to the important messages.

*Exercise:* Think of someone you've met in the last day or two. Can you give the following information about the person: eye color? height? color of their shirt? approximate age? name? How would you characterize their mood or state of mind at the time you met them?

Now, think of someone you see daily who is not a close friend. This might be the person who sells newspapers on the corner, the counter person at your local coffee shop, the person who asks for change outside your work. Can you answer the same questions about them?

*Activity:* The next time you go out for dinner, pay attention when the server announces, "My name is

So-and-so, and I'll be your server tonight." Then use the server's name when you address him or her. (A variation on this activity is to read the name tags many retail workers wear and address them by name.) Note: Ironically, using a person's name in this context is unusual enough that some people may be taken aback by it. To minimize this effect, try using the name when thanking them or requesting help: 'Thank you, Susan." "Excuse me, James, could you please bring me another glass of juice?"

---

*Exercise*: How can you tell if a person is angry? Depressed? Excited? List five non-verbal cues for each emotion.

---

**Suggested Reading: *How to Read a Person Like a Book* by Gerald I. Nierenberg and Henry H. Calero is the classic book on body language. Note that their study focuses on white Americans; people of other cultures and ethnic groups within the United States and abroad may use other cues.**

---

*Activity:* Go to a busy public place, like an outdoor café or a park. Close your eyes. Using your other senses, locate the person who is physically closest to you. What can you say about that person? Can you identify their gender, age, or ethnicity? What can you say about their voice? Can you smell perfume or some other scent? How heavy is their tread? Based on the information you gather, how would you describe this person? Now open your eyes. How accurate was your assessment?

This activity will teach you three important things: first, to use your senses to their fullest; second, to be aware of the limitations of your senses; and third, to notice the extent to which your assumptions can influence what you perceive and how you interpret sensory input.

> *Suggested Reading: Developing Creative and Critical Thinking: An Integrated Approach* **by Robert Boostrom is a textbook that can easily be used outside of the classroom. It will help you sharpen your observation skills and hone your mental abilities.**

# Lesson 9. Obedience III: self-discipline

In Lesson 7, you learned some self-observation skills. In the process, you may have discovered some things about yourself that you'd like to change. Perhaps you found that you slump. Or you chew your nails. Or you chatter when you get nervous.

Not only are these habits inappropriate for a slave, but in dealing with them early on in your training, you will gain the added benefit of developing another vital skill: self-discipline.

*Activity:* Continue to practice the focusing meditation described in Lesson 7. Meditate for ten minutes daily, and gradually increase your practice until you are meditang for twenty minutes at a sitting, twice a day.

*Exercise:* Name five individuals who embody the virtue of self-discipline for you. (They may be public figures or people known to you personally.) What can you learn from them?

*Suggested Reading:* **Read a biography of one of your personal models for self-discipline. Note the challenges that person faced and how he or she overcame them.**

# Lesson 10. Slave journal: the discipline of self-disclosure

By now you will have started to develop the skills necessary to name your emotions and needs more clearly. These skills have an outer and an inner component. On the outer side, you will be better able to inform your trainer of any difficulties that arise and will be able to answer probing questions about your current state of mind. On the inner side, you will also be cultivating for yourself the habit of Self-Observation. Increased awareness of your own motivations and thought patterns can be, in and of itself, a source of satisfaction.

The present lesson provides yet another technique for communicating with your trainer and working out your own processes.

Starting this week, you will keep a written account of your life in the form of a slave journal.

If you are working with a trainer, you will be turning over your journal to that person at regular intervals for evaluation. The journal is a document of your experience, and as such, nothing in it can be "right" or wrong" *per se.* It can be more or less detailed, more or less accurate, more or less honest, but it cannot be more or less correct. The only way you can fail at keeping a slave journal is by not writing in it.

*Activity:* Buy a special notebook or diary to use as a slave journal. It need not be fancy or expensive, although if a blank bound book is within your means, you may find it lends an aura of gravity to the act of writing. But even if your slave journal is a 99-cent spiral-bound notebook, it is an important facet of your training. You should also make sure that you have a pen (not a pencil) with which you can write easily for half an hour.

What should you write in your journal? Entries need not be long, and they do not even have to relate directly to the training process. What is important is the regularity with which you write and the effort you put into naming your emotions and experiences.

*Activity:* Review the affirmations exercise in Lesson 1. Use one of the suggested sentences or compose one of your own. Before you begin to write, kneel down (as you are able) for a minute and clear your mind. Visualize yourself speaking openly and honestly with your trainer or Owner whom you trust implicitly. Imagine that person responding firmly, but with deep understanding and care. Now, repeat your chosen affirmation: I devote myself to service. I serve for my benefit and that of others. By serving, I fulfill my highest calling. Then write in your journal. When you have finished, repeat your afirmatlon quietly to yourself.

*Exercise:* This exercise is for slaves who wish to use the slave journal as a preliminary tool leading to voice-training. Do not use it until you have been writing regularly for at least one month.

Try writing in your journal without using the capital "I" to refer to yourself. You may want to substitute the lower-case letter "i" at first. Later, you may want to avoid personal pronouns and possessives altogether:

this slave spent the day cleaning Mistress's boots and was content. This can lead to some interesting challenges: if you cannot say "my Master," what do you say? List three possible solutions to this problem.

---

*Suggested Reading:* **Written to help creatively blocked artists, Julia Cameron's best-selling book, *The Artist's Way*, contains some words of wisdom on journaling that those who keep slave journals will no doubt find helpful.**

# Lesson 11. Voice-training I: silence

It may seem ironic, but the first step in voice-training is learning when not to speak. For slaves, this will be most of the time. Slaves, like the children in the old saw, are to be "seen and not heard." For a slave, speech is a privilege, not a right.

If you have been working at the meditation practice suggested in earlier lessons, you are becoming more accustomed to silence. We live in a frightfully noisy world, and it is important for you as a slave-in-training to be able to filter out background distractions and focus on the task at hand. Developing inner silence is one effective technique to accomplish this.

Another is the simple practice of choosing silence.

---

*Exercise:* Sit quietly in your home with a pen and paper. For five minutes, just listen, as if you were listening to a piece of music. Then write down everything you can remember hearing.

---

*Activity:* At least once during this week, consciously choose silence. If you are accustomed to chatting with co-workers during your lunch break, eat out or go to the park. If you suffer a petty insult on the street, do not respond. If you are tempted to make a cutting remark, stop. Say nothing. Just once. If you usually listen to the radio in the car or watch television in the evening, take a day off. Notice how external silence helps you focus on the internal voices, and eventually, to quiet them as well.

# Lesson 12. Voice–training II: forms of address

Whether they realize it or not, most slaves do have a certain level of voice-training. Every time they say "Master," or "Mistress," "Sir," or "Ma'am," they are responding to the spoken or unspoken rules that dictate the way a slave speaks to an Owner or trainer.

*Exercise:* List all the titles of authority you can think of: Sir, Mistress, Officer, Majesty.... In non-scene life, what dictates when you use such a title? What cues (verbal or non-verbal) tell you to show respect by using a title? Is it possible to be disrespectful while using a formal title? What titles have you been called?

*Exercise:* Select a title that denotes dominance to you, and for one week, address your slave journal entries to that figure of authority. Do you find that your tone changes? Are there things you neglect or choose not to write? Why or why not?

*Suggested Reading:* Any secretarial handbook will list political, academic, and military forms of address. Familiarize yourself with them. (Note that the form used to address the individual directly sometimes differs from the form used in correspondence or when referring to someone indirectly.)

# Lesson 13. Personal care and fitness for slaves

When you spend a great deal of time caring for the needs and desires of others, it is all too easy to forget to care for yourself. How many times have you seen a tired, haggard mother with picture-perfect children? If you don't care properly for yourself, physically as well as psychologically, you'll have precious little to offer a dominant.

So no matter how pretty your manners, how manifold your accomplishments, if you are lacking in matters of personal hygiene, you will not go far as a slave. Slaves cannot afford to be overly fussy in matters of appearance, but they neglect the basics of the toilette at their peril.

Remember that your own appearance reflects on your trainer or Owner, so don't forget the following grooming basics:

- Frequent showers or baths with a good, effective soap;
- Clean hair, whatever the style;
- Appropriate use of deodorant/antiperspirant for your body chemistry and activity level;
- Clean, trimmed nails;
- Clean teeth and fresh breath;
- Clean, pressed clothing in good repair.

*Exercise:* List all of the personal care products you use: soap, shampoo, toothpaste, moisturizer, shaving cream....

*Activity:* If you use only the most basic grooming aids (soap, shampoo, and toothpaste, say), indulge in some bath oil or a scented soap. If you have more shades of lipstick than the Queen has jewels, try spending a weekend using just the basics.

---

*Activity:* Treat yourself to a manicure, pedicure, facial, or massage (or all of these) at a day spa or salon. Alternatively, you can create a spa experience for yourself at home. See *The Wellness Center's Spa at Home* by Kalia Doner and Margaret Doner for tips. Not only will a day of pampering make you feel delicious, you will also learn both how to care for yourself and how to perform some important "body service" tasks as well.

---

Basic fitness is also important for a slave. This isn't fitness for its own sake, but fitness for the tasks at hand. A light exercise program focusing on flexibility and balance is very helpful for a slave. A brisk daily walk and some simple stretches or yoga postures will do wonders for both your body and your spirit. However, as dominants' needs vary, so do slaves' physical abilities. You don't need to be an Olympic athlete – or for that matter, completely able-bodied – to serve, so don't allow fitness to become an obsession or a cause for self-deprecation.

---

*Activity:* Rent or purchase an exercise video that teaches basic stretches or yoga. Establish a simple exercise regime for yourself: a walk around the park, some deep knee bends and shoulder rolls.... If you work at a desk, be sure to get up at least once every thirty minutes to avoid tension and injury.

---

For further training, see the lessons on shaving and cleansing enemas and douches. For information on body service, see the Lady's Maid & Valet sections in "Area Studies."

*Suggested Reading:* if you're unfamiliar with men's grooming, read *Paisley Goes with Nothing*, pp. 101-134, for a concise and witty presentation of the basics. Men's magazines like *GQ* and *Details* offer grooming tips as well. in our culture, women are all too often inundated with advice on how to make themselves more attractive, most of it rubbish. Beyond the basics of cleanliness, sufficient sleep, and good posture, forget everything you've read about the wonders of cosmetics. What holds for men, holds for you, with or without Miraculous Anti-Wrinkle Gel.

# Lesson 14. Positioning the body: waiting and at rest postures

Ask experienced slaves what occupies most of their time, and they will tell you, "waiting." Along with the mental habits of mindfulness, observance, and quiet, slaves must train themselves to wait gracefully. Fidgeting is unbecoming in a slave. Luckily (if you will), modern life affords us all ample opportunity to practice our waiting skills.

---

*Activity:* The next time you find yourself waiting – in line at the supermarket, on hold on the telephone – try this simple exercise.

Observe your body and adopt an alert but relaxed posture. If you are standing, try moving your legs apart slightly so that you can balance evenly on both legs, rather than shifting your weight from side to side. Keep your knees slightly bent, not straight.

Now, quiet your mind by breathing slowly and evenly. (If you have been meditating regularly, this process will have become almost second nature.) Allow your eyes to maintain a soft focus on the floor approximately six feet in front of you.

Repeat your chosen affirmation to yourself silently.

One of the most common errors slaves-in-training make is to fidget with their hands. This next activity will help you become aware of your hands.

*Activity:* Stand with your weight balanced evenly on both feet, remembering to keep your knees bent ever-so-slightly. Allow your arms to hang comfortably at your sides. Consciously tense your hands by balling them into fists, and then release. Your now relaxed hands will naturally form a gently curved "cup" shape. (Pianists will recognize this as the correct hand position for keyboards as well.)

Now sit down on a straight-backed chair and rest your hands palms-down on your thighs. Notice that your hands will form the same "cup" shape. Now turn your hands palms up, Again, they retain the natural shape when relaxed, without stress or strain on the arms or wrists. This is a pretty, receptive posture and should be adopted when sitting or kneeling.

*Activity:* Stand and hold your arms behind your back with your hands together over the base of your spine. You may have to hold one of your wrists with the other hand. See how long you can maintain this posture without fatigue.

*Activity:* Kneel on a soft surface (like a rug or folded bath towel). Rest your buttocks on your ankles.

(This is sometimes called 'kneeling down," as opposed to "kneeling up" with your upper body at a right angle to your lower legs.) Position your hands in the receptive posture described above and lower your head so that your gaze falls on the floor about four feet in front of you. Try to stay in this position for five minutes without moving. (The "waiting exercise" given above may help you.)

---

*Safety Warning:* **If you have knee problems or feel any pain when kneeling, do not do it. Practice standing instead. Always be sure to inform your trainer if you experience any physical discomfort from a posture.**

# Lesson 15. Voice commands and body positions

Slaves must be able to respond to verbal commands without hesitation. If you are asked to move, you should do so quickly, but gracefully. Do not run unless specifically commanded to, as it greatly increases the risk of accidents.

If you are working with a trainer, you will be drilled until you can respond to voice commands with ease. If you are working independently, the following activity will help you.

---

*Activity:* Using a blank cassette tape and a tape recorder, make a tape that includes the following commands: Come here, go, attend, present, open, down, worship, wait. Wind the tape forward, then speak one of the commands into the recorder. Wind the tape forward again a space, then speak another command. Try to vary the order of the commands as well as the length of time between them. You may also want to give two or more commands in quick succession. When you are finished, you can play the tape and assume each position as you hear it. (Please be sure to do some basic stretches before you begin to avoid straining yourself.) Obviously you should only practice at home or in some other private place. (For the "come here" command, approach a specific chair; for "go," face the same chair and exit the room without turning your back on the chair. Practice both walking and crawling.)

---

*Activity:* Record a second tape, but this time speak the commands more rapidly, one after the other. Allow approximately three seconds between commands. (Count one one thousand, two one thousand, three one thousand silently between commands.) With practice, you will be able to move gracefully from one position to the next. You may find it helpful to practice in front of a mirror. Try the exercise naked as well.

---

*Activity:* After you've been working with the command tapes or a while, try videotaping yourself as you assume the various positions. You should work toward smooth, fluid movements without jerks or stops.

---

**Resources:** If you are not used to much physical activity, you may want to take a stretching or beginning yoga class. There are many exercise videos available to home use as well; choose one that emphasizes flexibility.

*Safety Warning:* If you experience pain during these exercises, stop. Be sure to do some simple stretches before you begin to minimize the chances of pulling a muscle.

# Lesson 16. Exploring feelings about punishment

As we near the end of the Basic Training section, we turn to one of the more troubling topics: punishment. Few people enjoy punishment for its own sake; some find it exciting in the context of erotic role-play. Nevertheless, most slaves will see the importance of some form of discipline as a pedagogical aid.

All punishment need not be corporal: in fact, I have found physical punishment to be among the least effective tools, as it tends to throw the slave into a vat of roiling emotions (many of them shadows of childhood) that make it impossible for the slave to think clearly. Corporal punishment does hold an important place in many people's erotic imaginations, and so maintains its place among the many forms of punishment a trainer or Owner may impose upon a wayward slave.

I do not suggest that punishments *per se* be imposed slaves until they have completed at least the most basic aspects of training. This is for the simple reason that, unless slaves have been taught what exactly is expected of them, they can't be held accountable if they fail to live up to a trainer's standards. Slaves aren't mind readers, after all. Hence the delay in attending to this delicate, albeit important, matter.

---

*Exercise:* Choose the answer that most accurately reflects your feelings.

1. You discover that you have made an error in a report that could cause your company to lose a significant amount of business. What do you do?
   a. I run off a errata slip to be included with the report, and give it to the person sending out the mailing.
   b. I inform my supervisor of the error immediately.

    c.   I stay late to retype the report.

    d.   I say nothing and pray the error won't be noticed. But I worry for weeks about the consequences.

2. When I was a child and my parents found out I'd broken a rule, they...

    a.   my parents? They were too busy to notice anything.

    b.   wanted to understand why I'd done it.

    c.   sometimes gave me weird punishments that didn't fit the crime.

    d.   said nothing, but gave me disappointed looks for days afterward.

3. The most important thing for children is that they...

    a.   be allowed freedom, but with clear limitations.

    b.   be encouraged to share their feelings and doubts.

    c.   be treated fairly.

    d.   be given lots of attention and love.

4. The hardest punishment for me to take would be...

    a.   being publicly disgraced.

    b.   being yelled at.

    c.   being sent away.

    d.   being ignored.

5. I think the worst thing a slave can do is...

    a.   get caught doing something wrong.

    b.   not communicate with the Owner.

    c.   not take steps to correct an error.

    d.   talk back to the Owner.

6. The stupidest punishment I've ever experienced was...

    a.   being grounded.

    b   having to write some dumb sentence about eight million times.

    c.   being spanked.

    d.   being given the silent treatment.

7. It would be easy for me to...

    a.   listen to a lecture on what I did wrong. At least I'd understand the problem better.

    b.   confess wrongdoing to the Owner. At least I'd have done the right thing morally.

    c.   have to re-do a task. At least I'd know how to do it better the next time.

    d.   deal with being physically punished. At least it's over right away.

8. When I was punished as a child, I mostly felt...

    a.   angry.

    b.   embarrassed.

    c.   dumb.

    d.   ashamed.

9. In slave training, I think punishment is...

    a.   a necessary evil.

    b.   a last resort.

    c.   one of the ways a slave learns.

    d.   one of the things I fear most.

And one more question:

10. I am...

    a.   a happy masochist.

    b.   open to exploring my masochistic fantasies.

    c.   not thrilled about the idea of physical punishment.

    d.   not into the SM side of things at all.

Now, count the number of times you chose (a), (b), (c), and (d) for questions 1-9.

If you chose mostly (a) answers, you tend to be sure of yourself and your abilities. You'll admit to making a mistake if pressed, but you'd rather just quietly cover your tracks and move on. Why rock the boat? is your motto. You may have grown up in a busy household, so you learned to handle crises for yourself. You tend to focus on the end result, not the means. You may have a hard time if you are punished for philosophical or ethical reasons, especially if no obvious harm resulted from your actions.

If you chose mostly (b) answers, you are not often in charge and prefer to have a superior to confer with. You probably have good verbal skills and are considered a "team player." When you make a mistake, the first thing you do is go back over your actions step by step until you uncover the "false move." For you, the process is at least as important as the end result. If you are reprimanded, you want to know what, specifically, you did wrong and how to avoid the same error in the future.

If you chose mostly (c) answers, you tend toward perfectionism. You want to see an error corrected at all costs. You may tend to overemphasize your intellectual side and may respond to punishment by berating yourself. You may judge yourself by unrealistically high standards, and it's hard for you to let someone else judge you, particularly if their standards differ from yours. You value fairness and balance, so you want to see the punishment fit the crime. Consequently, you may find corporal punishment frustrating or degrading.

If you chose mostly (d) answers, you tend to stew over errors you make, but are afraid to admit them, fearing the worst. As a result, your self-esteem suffers. You may have grown up in an authoritarian household, or your parents may have been emotionally distant. You may suffer from fear of abandonment. It is very difficult for you to confess wrong-doing, but you find it cathartic to do so. You crave positive reinforcement and supportive attention. If you are physically punished, you need reassurance that you have not failed totally.

If your answers were evenly divided between several letters, take note of any insights you may have gained from the exercise. What do you most fear about punishment? What childhood memories does it evoke? What, in your view, is the role of punishment in slave training?

You may wonder how question 10 fits into this scheme. Devising punishments for masochists remains a perennial problem for slave trainers. Unlike other submissives, masochistic slaves-in-training rarely derive benefit from corporal punishment, since they experience pleasure in intense sensation.

The solution, of course, is either to punish masochists with a type of sensation they dislike or to avoid corporal punishment altogether.

If you are working independently, this lesson will have served as an exercise in greater self-knowledge. Miss Abernathy cautions you against self-inflicted punishments, as it is all too easy to lose perspective. Instead, note your shortcomings in your slave journal.

# Lesson 17. The collar

The collar is the symbol *par excellence* of slavehood. It is an outward symbol of your state of servitude and of your Owner's (or trainer's) care for you. Unlike the slave journal, which legally and morally is yours, the collar remains the possession of the Owner and must be surrendered upon demand.

Since it is such a potent sign of a slave's position, the choice of collar is a delicate one. While you, as property, have no direct say in the style of the collar – that is for your trainer or Owner to decide – it may prove useful for you to think, in theoretical terms at least, about the collar as symbol.

*Exercise:* Write a paragraph describing your dream collar. What kind of material is it made of? Does it lock?

Does it include a tag ("This slave owned by...")? Could you wear this collar in non-scene public? Why or why not? How would others respond to seeing you in this collar? What feelings would the collar evoke in you?

---

*Activity:* Make a list of five substitutes for the traditional black leather slave collar. Try wearing one of these substitutes for a day. How does it make you feel? Do you find yourself aware of the collar? Of yourself as a slave-in-training?

---

**Safety Warning:** Take care that the item you choose does not obstruct your breathing; this is especially important if you want to sleep in the collar or perform hard physical labor or exercise, as your neck may swell.

---

*Activity:* Visit a shop that sells slave collars and try some on.

# Household Management

It is my assumption that most slaves will be engaged in some form of domestic service. In this day and age, however, it is impossible to make any assumptions about a slave's preparedness for this kind of work, regardless of age or gender. Further, housekeeping standards and needs vary so greatly from person to person that it is difficult to predict what any one dominant might require of you. Therefore, in this section I have undertaken a thorough discussion – perhaps, for some individuals, a review – of the rudiments of household management.

For the purposes of this section of the book, I will assume that you are the sole servant on hand and that the household in your care is of such size that no other help would be needed. Likewise, I assume that your Owner has turned over all basic household responsibilities to you and takes no active role, beyond the fiscal, in maintaining the household.

I strongly recommend that all slaves-in-training avail themselves of the information herein, even if they have no expectation of becoming house servants. Most dominants are busy people and would be delighted to find a slave who is as competent in the kitchen as in the bedroom. Further, some dominants will assess potential slaves by employing them first as houseboys. If they pass muster and prove trustworthy, they may be invited to receive further training. (This is a common practice among professional dominants.)

> *Suggested Reading:* In addition to the specific volumes mentioned in the lessons themselves, all domestic servants should come to terms with the basics of time management. Despite their cumbersome titles, the following books may prove of assistance: *The Complete Idiot's Guide to Managing Your Time* by Jeff Davidson, and *The Overwhelmed Person's Guide to Time Management* by Ronni Eisenberg with Kate Kelly. I also suggest *Organizing for the Creative Person* by Dorothy Lehmkuhl and Dolores Cotte, with the caveat that you must consider your Owner's personality type along with your own as you follow the authors' plan. Finally, *Organizing Hints & Tips* by Cassandra Kent is a gem.

# Lesson 18. Housework I: basic cleaning

Like most of us in this day and age, dominants are busy people. Professional organizers and cleaning services proliferate in our cities as more and more people have less and less time. Add to this the fact that for many people, cleaning house is about as much fun as a trip to the dentist, and you'll begin to understand why many dominants expect slaves to be competent in housekeeping.

As a slave-in-training, you may surprised to find that cleaning someone else's house is a very different experience from cleaning your own. Instead of grousing, "How little cleaning can I get away with?" you will find yourself enjoying dusting baseboards and yes, doing windows. Why? Because service-oriented submissives derive satisfaction not only from a job well done, but from the very fact of having performed a task for someone whom they love and admire.

## Housecleaning

However noble your intentions, though, you may feel overwhelmed when faced with a house in (sometimes desperate) need of cleaning. In this lesson we will be looking at the steps you'll take to develop and execute a thorough cleaning plan. in addition, we'll be looking at some basic laundry techniques. (For more information on clothing care, please see the section on Valets and Lady's Maids in "Area Studies.")

*Activity:* Read through the following steps quickly, then follow them for the home you wish to clean. This may be, for the time being, your own home, or that of your trainer. If at anytime you find yourself feeling overwhelmed, take a moment to focus your mind with the meditation techniques described in the "Basic Training" section. You are not expected to complete all the steps in this activity in one session, nor even in one day, particularly if the home is large or its cleaning has been neglected.

1) Inventory the rooms. In this step, you walk from room to room and make notes on what needs cleaning. You'll want to note any special features of the room – high ceilings, French doors, antique rugs – that need special attention. You may find it helpful to sketch a diagram of the room, marking furniture, fixtures, and other details.

2) Go over your list room by room and see if there is anything you don't already know how to clean. Look up the information in a

good reference book (see the Bibliography
for Miss Abernathy's favorites).

3) Break the job into small, manageable tasks.
This step is vital to your success. If you
think, "I have to clean the entire house this
morning," you'll become disheartened and
run the risk of spending your time worrying
instead of cleaning. If you say, "I have to
dust the credenza right now," you'll be better
able to approach the task.

4) Gather your tools. Again, you may want
to refer to a book if you are unsure of what
you'll need. Consider environmentally
safe cleansers like vinegar, baking soda,
and lemon juice: They are not only more
pleasant to use, but you'll save money as
well. (See the lesson for Housekeepers for
some more ideas on "green" cleaning.)
Be sure to wear lined rubber gloves to
protect your skin, and if you must use
toxic chemicals, read and follow the safety
guidelines on the package.

5) Complete each task before moving to the next.
(A half-polished silver tea service is no more
useful than a completely tarnished one.)

6) Complete each room before moving to the
next. It is helpful to start your cleaning to
the right of the door you entered by and
work clockwise around the room until you
are finished.

7) Note down any difficulties you encounter
so you can search for alternative cleaning
methods. (For example, if you tried to clean

a bathtub with a non-abrasive cleanser, but found it didn't cut through the soap film, you will want to try an abrasive cleanser.) When you find a method that works particularly well, record it in a household journal.

8) To help you better plan your time, note how long each task takes. Many will become easier with practice, so don't be dismayed.

9) Finally, draw up a regular schedule for housecleaning. It should include tasks to be done daily, weekly, biweekly, monthly, semi-annually, and annually. For example, beds should be made daily, and sheets changed weekly, but mattresses need be turned only semi-annually. Scheduling will help you distinguish the more important tasks from the less. Most of the suggested books contain schedules that can be adapted to your specific needs.

**Suggested Reading: If there is only one reading suggestion you take, let it be this: Cassandra Kent's *Household Hints & Tips*. This invaluable guide shows you – with the aid of clear illustrations – how to handle everything from basic household deaning to artificial respiration. Second only to Kent are *Speed Cleaning* and *Spring Cleaning* by Jeff Campbell and the Clean Team.**

*Activity:* Hire a professional cleaning service to spring-clean your house. Watch how the cleaners work. (You will want to tell them that you'll be observing them "to pick up some cleaning tips" so they don't feel intimidated.) If hiring a service isn't an option for you, please read the *Clean Team* books cover to cover.

---

*Activity:* Many newspapers have a "household hints" column. Make a point of reading it regularly; clip or lot down any useful tips.

---

### Laundry

Along with housecleaning, most slaves in domestic service will be expected to attend to the household laundry. Whether you have access to a washer and dryer in the house or will be taking the laundry out, there are a few important factors to bear in mind.

1) Sort the laundry by color. Whites should be washed by themselves. Miss Abernathy prefers light and dark colors to be separated as well, rendering approximately three loads.

2) Read the labels on clothing to determine the types of fabrics. Most labels also have laundry instructions.

3) Select the water temperature and wash cycle based on the most delicate item in the load. You should use the hottest water that the fabrics can withstand. In general, whites should be washed in hot water, colors in warm, and any non-colorfast items in cold. All rinses can be in cold water.

4) Do not use too much detergent, especially in industrial washers which often contain the residue of previous users' soap. It is not the suds that clean clothes, but the (often invisible) cleansers and borax in the detergent. In fact, many products contain a sudsing agent only because consumers expect to see suds. These sudsing agents are not only unnecessary but may be harmful to the environment.

(For information on treating stains on clothing, consult Cassandra Kent's *Household Hints & Tips*.)

5) Bleach should be used sparingly, as it is caustic and causes fibers to weaken. Always dilute bleach in water and then add clothes. Do not use liquid bleach on colors; choose a powder specifically designed for use on colors.

6) If you use fabric softener, it should be added to the rinse cycle. (Note that fabric softeners can be irritating to the skin because of the perfumes they contain. If you are doing laundry for a person with allergies or sensitive skin, choose an unperfumed softener or skip it altogether.)

7) Dry each load separately (do not mix whites with colors). Again, choose the highest temperature the clothing can withstand: high for cottons, medium for permanent press, low for more delicate fabrics.

8) Remove clothes from the dryer as soon as they are finished to avoid wrinkling. Clothes that will be ironed should be hung on hangers. All other items should be folded and put away immediately. Some people are very particular about how their clothes are folded. If you are in doubt, ask, or check their drawers for examples of properly folded garments.

9) If you are drying clothes on a line outdoors, they may become stiff. A quick once-over with a warm iron will soften the fabric again.

10) Before ironing, check the garment label for specific instructions. Also check the iron before you turn it on to make sure it is clean. Cotton and linen clothes require a very hot iron, and you may need to spritz the clothes with plain water, too. (If your water contains a lot of minerals – "hard water" – use distilled or filtered water to avoid mineral stains on clothes.)

11) Ironing is not difficult, but it does require some patience and practice. Consult any of the Suggested Reading books for hints on ironing.

12) Finally, do not attempt to deal with clothing marked "dry clean only" by yourself. Turn them over to a professional dry cleaner. (For more information on caring for fine dress clothes, see the lesson on Ladies' Maids and Valets.)

Some fabrics (most silks and fine wools) and certain garments (stockings and other lingerie) must be washed by hand. Fill a clean sink with cool water. While the water is running, add a small amount of mild washing soap. Immerse the garments in the soapy water one at a time and squeeze the suds through the garments. Do not scrub or wring the garments. Rinse with fresh water and hang to dry. Sweaters and other items that might become misshapen if hung should be "blocked" on a drying rack. (Avoid wooden racks, as they may splinter and often decay with prolonged exposure to dampness.)

---

*Activity:* Organize your sock drawer so that you can locate any individual pair of socks by touch only. Hint: separate socks by color and weight. Use old shoe boxes or tissue boxes to separate the categories.

---

*Exercise:* Right now, how many pairs of clean underwear do you have on hand? When you are caring for a dominant's clothing, it is important to make sure that several days' worth of outfits are in the wings at all times. Don't procrastinate with the washing. If you include laundry in your regular cleaning schedule, it will not build up and become burdensome.

---

**Dishes**

Finally, even if they are not cooking or eating in the house, slaves are frequently called upon to wash dishes. If you have the use of an electric dishwasher, you will find this a simple task. Rinse the dishes to remove any large pieces of food, then load glassware and anything marked "upper rack dishwasher safe" (some plastics) in the upper rack, and plates, pots, and pans in the lower rack. Add the dishwashing detergent (powder or liquid), close the machine, and turn it on. What could be simpler?

If you are washing dishes by hand, however, the task involves a bit more planning. Be sure to wear lined rubber gloves to spare your hands. Using hot water and dishwashing liquid, wash glassware first, then cutlery, then plates, then any pots and pans or greasy utensils. Be sure to rinse the soap off carefully, as soap that has dried on dishes can cause gastrointestinal disturbances if ingested. Pots and pans with baked-on food or burned bottoms should be soaked in hot water with a little soap for 15-20 minutes, then washed thoroughly. You may need to use an abrasive sponge or steel wool to remove the burned food, but be sure that the pan will not be damaged by abrasion. (Heatproof glass pans and pans with non-stick coatings are delicate and should be handled with care.)

Crystal and silver should never be washed in a dishwasher. When washing crystal, put a terry cloth towel in the bottom of the sink to avoid chipping the crystal, and only use warm water. Silver should be dried immediately and stored in felt bags to minimize tarnishing.

Some fine china must also be washed by hand. Use the same technique as with crystal.

---

*Activity:* If you are accustomed to washing your dishes in a machine, try washing them by hand for a few days.

Some people find the repetitive nature of the task and the sound and feel of the warm water quite soothing.

# Lesson 19. Housework II: grocery and household shopping

Grocery shopping is another task that many dominants are happy to turn over to a slave. Like cleaning, it is not inherently difficult, but does require some planning.

### Shopping lists

Are you the sort of person who shops by wandering down the aisles and picking up whatever looks appetizing at the moment? Do you ever shop when you're hungry? Have you ever arrived home after a trip to the supermarket only to discover that you still don't have anything to eat for dinner? If you're nodding vigorously (or blushing), please read this section carefully.

*Exercise:* Ideally, you'll need the help of a friend for this activity. Make up a short shopping list (5-10 items), and send your friend to the store. What does she return with?

You may find that while you wrote "canned corn," you really meant a 12-ounce can of Del Monte canned corn... but you got a 6-ounce can of generic creamed corn. If you don't have the aid of a friend, list a few items you regularly buy (bread, milk, cereal...) and spend some time looking at the staggering variety of items available at your local supermarket. If you wrote "milk," for example, you'll find half-and-half, whole milk, reduced fat milk (1% and 2%), skim or non-fat milk, acidophilus milk, lactose-free milk, and goat's milk, not to mention powdered (instant) milk in both whole and non-fat varieties, evaporated milk and sweetened condensed milk. Obviously, the lesson here is: Be specific.

---

*Activity:* Go through the cupboards of the kitchen you'll be shopping for (perhaps your own) and make a list of each and every item you find, including the size and brand names. Add to this list anything that you normally keep on hand but might be out of at the moment. Include spices, baking supplies, and other items that you may use infrequently. Then do the same for the refrigerator. (While you're at it, throw away any perishables that are making your kitchen look like a science lab.) Now check your cleaning and paper supplies and any toiletries and add any appropriate items to your list. You have just created a Master Shopping List.

---

**Suggested Reading: If you are just beginning to stock a kitchen, refer to *Bride's Lifetime Guide to Good Food and Entertaining,* p. 6, or *Dad's Own Cookbook* by Bob Sloan, pp. 21-22, for lists of staples.**

---

*Activity:* Go to your usual supermarket with a pad of paper and a pencil. Draw a box to represent the store and divide the box into columns to represent the aisles. In each column, write the items displayed in each aisle: produce, dairy, frozen foods, baking products, cereal.... General headings are all you need; use the overhead signs in the aisles if you need help.

Now, match up the specific items on your Master Shopping List with the schematic drawing of the supermarket. The result will look something like this:

| Produce | Paper Products | Frozen Foods |
|---|---|---|
| bananas | Brand X toilet paper | store brand frozen peas |
| apples | Brand Q paper towels | Len & Larry's Quadruple |
| salad greens | Brand Z tissues (white)... | Chocolate ice cream... |
| fresh basil... | | |

Leave some blank spaces at the end for items you may have forgotten.

Photocopy your store-diagram-cum-shopping-list and hang one copy on the refrigerator or on the inside of a cupboard door, along with a small pencil. When you run out of an item, circle it on the list. When you're ready to shop, take the list with you. It will help you speed through the store. (For information on using menus to plan your grocery shopping trips and tips on household budgeting and shopping, see "The Housekeeper" in the Area Studies section.)

This system can be adapted for most stores, including drugstores, office supply stores, and large chain variety stores. The initial time investment will prove minimal compared to the savings of time and money you'll enjoy using this shopping method.

*Resources:* **Some supermarkets now offer computer-assisted grocery shopping. They provide software – a database of their stock – that allows you to select the items you want (and alternatives). You submit your list by e-mail and specify a delivery time. While this service can be costly, it does allow you to look at a store's offerings systematically and can be invaluable for those for whom shopping or transporting groceries is difficult.**

# Lesson 20. Housework III: basic cooking

Remember the old saying that the way to a man's heart is through his stomach? Male or female, most dominants appreciate a well-prepared meal. In addition to providing energy and nutrients for our bodies, food nourishes the soul. It can be a source of comfort as well as pleasure. What better way to care for someone than to prepare a feast for their senses?

**Basic skills**

Virtually anyone can learn the basics of cooking. If you can read and follow directions, you can cook. If you're not yet comfortable in the kitchen, take some time to read about food.

*Activity:* Purchase or borrow a copy of one of the basic cookbooks on the *Suggested Reading* list. Don't worry about making any of the recipes yet: Just read the cookbook as a book. Note any terms or ingredients that are unfamiliar to you and make a point of finding more information on them. (*The Joy of Cooking* and *Le Cordon Bleu Complete Cooking Techniques* are good secondary reference books.)

*Activity:* Buy and read a cooking magazine or two. *Cook's Illustrated* is a fine publication for the beginner.

*Activity:* Inventory your cooking tools. You may own a single skillet and a tea kettle or a 25-piece set of professional grade cookware. List everything you have on hand. (If you will be cooking elsewhere, inventory that kitchen instead.)

*Activity:* Cable stations often run high-quality cooking shows by well-known chefs; the Food Network runs them nearly around-the-clock. Check your local programming, and watch a few. You can also record them for later viewing.

*Activity:* If you learn best by doing, rather than reading or watching, try taking a hands-on course. Community centers and adult schools offer low-cost cooking classes.

## Simple classic meals

At minimum, a slave should know how to make a few classic dishes. None of these meals takes more than an hour, including cooking time. The ingredients are all readily available at your supermarket, and the recipes – which serve at least two – can be doubled if needed. Be sure to check beforehand to see if anyone you'll be cooking for has food allergies, a dislike for any of the main flavors, or other special dietary needs.

### Breakfast Muffins
1 c. flour (white or wheat)
1 c. instant oatmeal
1/4 c. sugar
2 t. baking powder
1/2 t. salt (optional)
1 c. milk
1/4 c. vegetable oil
1 egg
1 c. raisins, shredded coconut, nuts, berries, or chopped apple (optional)

Preheat the oven to 400°F. Combine dry ingredients in a bowl, then mix in wet ingredients, stirring until iust combined (batter will be lumpy). Fill greased muffin tins 2/3 full. Bake approximately 20 minutes or until golden brown. Makes 1 dozen.

Variations: Substitute 3/4 c. cornmeal or crushed flake cereal for the oatmeal and increase the flour to 1 1/2 c.

### Onion Soup

2 T. butter or margarine
4 c. thinly sliced onions
6 c. broth (vegetable or beef)
1/4 c. dry red wine
1/2 t. dried thyme
1/4 t. dried savory
1 bay leaf
salt and pepper to taste

Melt the butter in a large saucepan and sauté onions at medium heat until soft. Add remaining ingredients and bring to a boil. Simmer uncovered for 1 hour. Remove and discard bay leaf before serving. Serves 6 as a first course.

Variations: While the alcohol in the red wine will cook out of the soup, if you are cooking for someone who does not tolerate alcohol well, substitute 2 T. soy sauce and omit the salt.

For a simple, hearty lunch, spoon soup into an oven-safe bowl over a slice of day-old French bread. Top with grated parmesan or romano cheese and a slice of Swiss or fontina cheese. Place bowl under a broiler until the cheese is melted.

### Angel Hair Pasta with Tomato Sauce
1 large (28-oz.) can diced tomatoes
4 medium peeled, chopped garlic cloves
3 T. olive oil (extra virgin is best)
2 T. coarsely chopped fresh basil leaves
1/4 t. sugar
1 1/2 t. salt
3/4 lb. capellini (angel hair)

Sauté the garlic in the olive oil until fragrant. Before the garlic turns brown, add the tomatoes and cook until thickened a bit (approx. 10 minutes). Add the basil, sugar, and salt. Cook for an additional 10 minutes.

While sauce is cooking, cook the pasta in a large pot of boiling, salted water. Capellini cooks very quickly (2 minutes); other noodles take longer. Check the package. Do not overcook the pasta; it should be al dente – firm to the bite.

Drain the pasta in a colander and add it to the sauce. Cook for 1 minute, then serve immediately with freshly grated parmesan or cheese. Serves 3, or 2 very hearty eaters.

Variations: This basic dish can be varied by including ground beef and/or veal in the sauce (brown the meat in a skillet and drain away the fat before adding to the sauce), or lightly sautéed zucchini and onions.

### Roast Chicken with Vegetables
1 large roasting chicken with innards removed
8 cloves peeled garlic
1/2 t. dried thyme
8 new red potatoes, washed

2 carrots, washed, peeled, and cut into 2-inch long hunks

1 large onion

olive oil

Preheat oven to 350°F. Wash the chicken carefully and place it breast up in a baking dish. Chop the onion and combine it with the thyme, and a little olive oil. Stuff the chicken with the mixture. Cut small slits in the skin of the breast and put one garlic clove in each. Brush olive oil over the surface of the bird. Arrange potatoes and carrots around the chicken. Place pan in oven and bake until done (approximately 1 hour). To check doneness, cut into the breast with a knife down to the bone. If the chicken is white all the way through (no pink showing), it is done.

Variations: Substitute dill for the thyme. Try other root vegetables like turnips or sweet potatoes instead of, or in addition to, the potatoes and carrots.

*Safety Warning:* **Always wash your hands and all utensils, including the cutting board, with soap, immediately after handling raw chicken or other meats.**

### Garlic Lover's Bread

1 loaf fresh Italian bread

8-10 cloves garlic, peeled and finely diced

1/8 lb. butter

1/8 c. extra virgin olive oil

dried parsley

Melt the butter and olive oil together and mix with the garlic.

Slice the bread lengthwise and spread with butter-oil-garlic mixture.

Sprinkle lightly with parsley. Put the two halves of the loaf back together and wrap in foil. Heat in a 400°F. oven for 15 minutes.

Unwrap and cut into 2-inch slices before serving. Serves 4-6.

Warning: This bread is a garlic lover's dream... but may be a nightmare for friends the next day. To cut the smell of garlic on the breath, drink a full glass of milk.

---

For a simple dessert, serve a scoop of vanilla ice cream in a dessert bowl topped with Grand Marnier, Bailey's Irish Cream, or raspberry jam that has been heated slightly.

---

*Activity:* Cook one or more of these dishes for yourself. If you enjoy them, begin a recipe file. Note any variations you try.

---

*Suggested Reading:* With literally thousands of cookbooks on the market, you could cook a different dish every night for the rest of your life and never get through them all. If you are a beginner, though, it is best to obtain one or two of the classic introductions to the art of cooking. Miss Abernathy favors *The Way to Cook* by the inimitable Julia Child, but the following titles will also stand you in good stead. *The New Making of a Cook* by Madeleine Kamman, *The Joy of Cooking* by Irma S. Rombauer, Marion Rombauer Becker and Ethan Becker (older editions may be preferable if you favor a classic approach), and *Le Cordon Bleu Complete Cooking Techniques* by Jeni Wright and Eric Treuillé. If you prefer American-style home cooking, you might try one of the *Fannie Farmer, Better Homes & Gardens,* or *Betty Crocker* cookbooks. Absolute beginners who only need to be able to make a few simple dishes might also enjoy *Dad's Own Cookbook* by Bob Sloan. For a list of books on wine, please see the reference book list in the chapter on Advanced Butlering.

## Drinks: coffee and tea

A slave's ability to make a decent cup of coffee or tea is priceless. Tastes in these drinks vary greatly from person to person, and indeed from region to region, so a slave does well to inquire about a dominant's preferences.

To make coffee, start with the correct grind for the brewing method you'll be using. In general, the finer the grind, the more flavorful the coffee. A standard proportion is one tablespoon of ground coffee to six ounces of cold water for coffee machines and filter or drip methods. Avoid percolators, as they often give a metallic or burned taste to the brew. Heat the water to boiling and then pour over the coffee, making sure to soak all the grounds. Coffee can be kept hot in a thermal carafe, but should not be left on the heating unit of a coffee machine, as it will scorch and taste foul.

Coffee is usually served with cream (half-and-half in the United States) or sometimes milk, and sugar and/or artificial sweetener. A tablespoon of liqueur can be added after dinner for a sweet dessert coffee. (Flavored coffees, although they smell lovely in the shop, are often weak and tasteless once brewed.)

Tea drinkers are perhaps even more particular about their brew than coffee aficionados. Whenever possible, use loose tea rather than tea bags for the best flavor. (Metal or mesh tea balls allow the tea to expand more and so yield a fuller flavor. They also have distinct environmental advantages.) The usual proportion for a pot of tea is "one teaspoon per cup and one for the pot." Again, start with cold water. For black tea, heat the water until it just boils: Look for small bubbles. (Despite the ubiquity of the teakettle, using a saucepan makes it easier to gauge the water temperature.) Pour the water over the tea to cover and allow to steep for 3-5 minutes. Green teas require slightly cooler water and a shorter steeping time. (If you're using loose tea placed directly into the pot, remember to strain the tea as you serve it.)

Pouring the tea is a distinction usually given to the (female) guest of honor. If you are asked to pour, remember that it is traditional to put the sugar and milk into the cup first and then pour the tea in. This is because many fine teacups are very thin and the hot tea might crack them. The cool milk absorbs the heat and saves the cup. (If you are serving tea in glasses or without milk, place a metal spoon in the glass to absorb the heat.)

Black tea may be served with milk (not cream, which is too heavy and obscures the subtle flavors of the tea), sugar, honey, or lemon. Never mix lemon and milk, as the milk will curdle. Green teas are served without any additions, often in small cups.

Never re-use tea by pouring more hot water over it. This is the equivalent of adding more hot water to a pot of brewed coffee. Cold, used tea bags make wonderful eye compresses and will also absorb strong odors in the refrigerator.

> *Suggested Reading:* The traditions surrounding afternoon tea are so rich and varied that they form the subject matter of numerous books. Among the best are *The Afternoon Tea Book* by Michael Smith, *The London Ritz Book of Afternoon Tea* by Helen Simpson, and *The Pleasures of Afternoon Tea* by Angela Hynes. All contain some background on the history of British teas as well as recipes and menu suggestions.

# Area Studies

Congratulations! You have completed the basic skills training and household management sections of the course and are moving into more specialized work. If you've taken care to complete the exercises up to this point, you are prepared to make some more informed decisions about the direction your training as a slave will take.

Early on in lesson 2, you were asked to take a brief diagnostic test to help you get some ideas about the different kinds of slaves and your own interests and natural abilities. Please review that lesson now, and re-take the test. You may find that after several months of training, you know yourself better and your ideas have changed. Note which type(s) of slavehood most appeal to you, and proceed to those areas below.

Even if you know beyond the shadow of a doubt that you want to be a sex slave or a lady's maid, please at least read through the information and exercises in the other sections. As I indicated in the introduction to the Household Management section, most slaves are expected to perform some type of domestic service, and it is to your benefit to have at least a working knowledge of what is required to run a house. Likewise, even if you already have a clear arrangement with a dominant that genital sex will never be a part of your relationship, you would do well to review the information in the lessons for sex slaves, as it contains ideas that may help you develop a more holistic view of sexuality. Again, congratulations on your work thus far.

# Sex Slaves

Sex is a natural part of being human. It exists both for reproductive purposes and for the joy it brings us. Many slaves-in-training first became aware of their submissive natures in a sexual context and for most, sex remains an important part of their experience of slavehood.

### Sex workers as role models

If you have chosen to focus your training on the sexual arena, you have much work ahead of you. Many beginners think being a sex slave is a life of leisure: after all, you have sex all the time, right? What could be better? Unfortunately, no one can have sex for hours and hours every day without it becoming tiresome, even boring. Ask any sex worker: sex is hard work.

In fact, sex workers are your role models now. Just as accountants deal with numbers and finances, and builders deal with materials, plans, and tools, sex workers deal – professionally, day in and day out – with sexuality, both their own and other people's. If they take their job seriously, and many do, they spend time and energy learning how to do that job better. They read and take classes, they talk shop with their peers, they form alliances and professional organizations.

At its best, sex work can become a spiritual calling, a vocation in the highest sense. Sex workers are healers and priestlesses. They take a powerful experience – sex – and use it to move themselves and others into ecstasy and communion with the divine. As a sex slave, you too can become a healer, a mediator of spiritual energy.

## Sex slave psychology

If you've led an active sex life thus far, you may be wondering what makes a sex slave different from any other healthy man or woman with a reasonably high sex drive. Is it just a matter of some play-acting?

What distinguishes a sex slave from any other lover is part of what distinguishes a houseboy from a professional domestic: attitude. While lovers may certainly derive satisfaction from pleasing their partners, they generally want to experience some pleasure for themselves. If that pleasure is denied, they will feel slighted, at very least, and may simply write off their partner as "selfish" or "not a very talented lover." A sex slave, on the other hand, makes him- or herself available for the dominant's pleasure with no expectation of physical gratification for themselves. Their satisfaction lies in serving, not in orgasm.

For a slave, sex is a service on par with cooking, cleaning, and personal attendance. It does not carry with it any greater respect than polishing boots, cooking a soufflé, or scrubbing the floor. It is service, period. It is important to recognize that all of these activities have equal value and require dedication, intelligence, and skill.

You should bear in mind, however, that to allow themselves to be served, dominants enter into a pact of trust with their slaves and must rely on their discretion and integrity. This is especially true of sex slaves, since physical intimacy is often equated with vulnerability in our sexual economy. Likewise, the slave must trust that the dominant has the slave's best interests and well-being in mind. In addition to the satisfaction of serving, you may eventually earn the honor of more complete trust from the dominant. For this you should strive.

## Self-care for sex slaves

Sex slaves need to attend to self-care, perhaps more than any other kind of slave. If you've been running around all day polishing silver, it's assumed you'll want to rest. It's easy to think that sex slaves live a life of leisure and pleasure and don't need any time to relax. Nothing could be further from the truth. Sexual energy is perhaps the most powerful we humans know and working with it can cause "burnout." Again, ask any sex worker.

As you work through this material, be sure to take plenty of time for yourself. Take frequent walks and long, soaking baths. Attend carefully to your meditation and consider yoga or tai chi to help balance your body and psyche. Because you may spend more time naked, you will want to pay special attention to your personal hygiene; some of the lessons below will cover personal care issues of special interest to sex slaves. Most of all, be sure to communicate with your trainer (as well as in your slave journal) about any emotional or physical changes that you experience.

## A note on safer sex

As part of your training contract, you may have negotiated an agreement about safer sex. As a sex slave, the practical aspects of safer sex may often be left to you. It behooves you to understand what types of sexual behaviors leave you and your partner(s) at risk for disease transmission and to take appropriate precautions. All of the general sex manuals and beginning SM books listed below will give you the basics of safer sex. Use them wisely. See also *The New Our Bodies, Ourselves* by the Boston Women's Health Book Collective and *Total Health for Men* ed. Neil Wertheimer. *The Complete Guide to Safe Sex* video is another good resource and covers all orientations as well as BDSM.

**Resources: San Francisco Sex Information provides referrals and information on sex-related topics by phone (not**

phone sex!). They are online at www.sfsi.org, or available afternoons and evenings by telephone at (415) 989-SFSI.

*Suggested Reading:* Begin with one or two general sex manuals. *The Good Vibrations Guide to Sex* by Cathy Winks and Anne Semans is down-to-earth, pansexual, and more woman-focused than some other books. *The Ultimate Sex Book* by therapist Anne Hooper is also copiously illustrated and relatively well-disposed toward erotic role-play. Although many of the techniques are not gender specific, the book maintains a definite heterosexual focus. *The (New) Our Bodies, Ourselves* is full of good information about female sexuality, and *The New Male Sexuality* contains similar information for and about men.

Many collections of sex tips are available. Among the best are Jay Wiseman's lighthearted *Tricks: To Please a Woman* and *Tricks: To Please a Man*, as well as *Sex Tips for Straight Women from a Gay Man* by Dan Anderson and Maggie Berman. Anything by Lou Paget is likely to be knowledgeable and helpful.

Some basic books on BDSM should also be part of any sex slave's library. *SM 101* by Jay Wiseman, *The Loving Dominant* by John Warren, *Sensuous Magic* by Patrick Califia, *Learning the Ropes* by Race Bannon, *Screw the Roses, Send Me the Thorns* by Miller and Devon, *Consensual Sadomasochism* by Henkin and Holiday, and *The Lesbian SM Safety Manual* ed. Califia, are all noteworthy for their sanity, readability, and emphasis on physical and emotional safety, not to mention the sheer volume of information between their covers.

Recent years have seen an upsurge in nonfiction about D/S and master/slave relationships. Jack Rinella has written *The Compleat Slave, The Master's Manual, Becoming a Slave* and others. Guy Baldwin's *SlaveCraft* is also worthy of study. These books will disagree with this one on some points, which just goes to prove that there are many ways to approach slavehood, and that the only final arbiters of correctness are you and your master or mistress.

Sex slaves should read all the erotica they can get their hands on, including "real life fantasy" collections like *His Secret Life* by Bob Berkowitz and *My Secret Garden and Women on Top* by Nancy Friday. While erotica is not always the best source for sex tips – some of what excites in print may be dangerous, illegal, or simply impossible in real life – it is an excellent resource for fantasy and gives the reader insight into the workings of the erotic imagination.

Finally, take the time to read some of the ground-breaking writing by and about sex workers that has appeared in the last few years. Self-aware and -empowered sex workers can be role models for sex slaves. *Whores and Other Feminists* ed. Jill Nagle, is a snappy and hard-hitting anthology of essays and personal narratives by self-identified feminist sex workers and their allies. Also recommended are *Paying For It* ed. Greta Christina, and *Sex Work: Writings by Women in the Sex Industry* by Frédérique Delacoste and Priscilla Alexander.

*Suggested Viewing:* There are many high quality sex education videos available; these aren't the mortifying "where babies come from" films you saw in health class. If you have difficulty finding any of these videos in your area, they can be purchased from Good Vibrations at

**www.goodvibes.com or by phone at 1-800-289-8423, 7
a.m.-7 p.m., Monday through Friday.**

# Lesson 21. Personal care I: shaving

For many people, shaving their pubic hair is highly erotic. Hairiness is sometimes considered "animal" or "virile" and equated with strong sex drive or an "active" role; hairlessness suggests vulnerability, a winning quality in a slave. A hairless pubis may also suggest youth and innocence. Shaving also makes visible that which is usually hidden and private, and some submissives enjoy the feeling of "complete nakedness" that shaving brings.

---

*Exercise:* Complete the following sentences.

When I imagine myself without pubic hair, I feel...

My hair is...

If I were shaved, I'd be embarrassed to...

Women with no pubic hair look...

Men with no pubic hair look...

As a slave, my pubic hair...

I'd shave, except...

If I were ordered to shave, I'd...

---

*Activity:* Remove your pubic hair by shaving or wax treatment. If you hair is very long or thick, trim it first with blunt-tipped scissors or electric dippers. Go slowly. Then soak in a warm tub for about fifteen minutes. This will open your pores and make shaving easier. Start with a new disposable safety razor. Apply a mild soap lather or shaving cream to the area and shave using short strokes in the same direction as the hair grows. (For the closest possible shave, you will need to shave against the direction of growth; save this for last.) You may need to pull looser skin taut and use a good magnifying mirror for areas you can't easily see. If you nick yourself, be sure to wash the area carefully and apply a dab of anti-bacterial ointment.

If you find you have strong negative feelings about being completely shaven, try just trimming your pubic hair. This will give you a neat appearance and is a good aid to hygiene. Women may want to experiment with the "ice cream cone cut," where the hair on the mons is trimmed short (often in a neat triangle or strip) and the hair on the outer labia is shaved.

You may experience some itching as the hair begins to grow back; apply talcum powder to the area to reduce the itch. Particularly if your hair is very curly, you'll want to wash the area daily with warm water, mild soap, and a terry washcloth to prevent ingrown hairs. (Some people prefer a loofah sponge; use it gently to avoid irritation.) People who shave regularly report that the itching becomes less bothersome as your skin adjusts to being shaved. If you find that shaving irritates your skin, you may want to try other depilation methods like waxing or hair removal creams. Visit a salon for help, or read the package instructions carefully if you're removing hair at home.

*Activity:* Experiment with shaving other parts of your body. Always begin with a fresh razor and lots of warm water.

# Lesson 22. Personal care II: cleansing enemas and douches

Enemas play a role in many people's sexual fantasies: the Naughty Nurse with her rolling enema cart is a popular dominant persona.

But aside from fantasy fulfillment, what practical reasons are there for using enemas? I see two functions that relate to slaves.

The primary reason is to make anal sex (including the use of anal plugs) more comfortable and aesthetically pleasing. Fecal matter contains bacteria and can be gritty, making anal sex both irritating to the rectum and potentially dangerous. Many people find the smell and sight of feces unpleasant, too. The solution: cleansing enemas.

The second reason enemas find their way into slave training is that many slaves find that receiving an enema, particularly when administered by a dominant, enhances their submission. Our culture attaches a great deal of shame to the anus, and allowing another person to control this part of the body can induce deeply submissive feelings.

It is important to remember that the bowel is quite delicate and must be treated with care. Cleansing enemas should be gently administered using warm water and low pressure. It usually takes no more than one quart of water to clean out the lower bowel for anal play.

Introduce the water slowly and pause if you feel any cramping. Give yourself plenty of time to release the water and waste, too.

> *Safety Warnings*: It isn't necessary to add anything to the water, and indeed, some additives are very dangerous. Alcohol in enemas can be fatal! The only exception to this rule is salt. Some people suggest dissolving one-half teaspoon or so of table salt in each quart of water to help replace the salts depleted by the enema process; several glasses of water or electrolyte-fortified "sports beverages" drunk after the process will also help balance fluids in the system.

While the occasional use of enemas isn't thought to be harmful, over-use can lead to weakened bowel function and dependence on enemas for elimination. High colonics also deplete important digestive flora; eat a cup of live-culture yogurt to replace them.

---

*Activity:* Purchase an enema bag – many are marketed as "hot water bottles with attachments." Assemble the bag and clean it before use by filling with warm water and one tablespoon of white vinegar (acetic acid solution). Let this solution run through the bag; repeat two more times with clean water.

Now you are ready to administer a cleansing enema. (Some people find it helpful to drink a cup of coffee first, as it stimulates the bowel, but this is not necessary.) Fill the bag with warm water (test it on the inside of your elbow) and hang no more than 6-8 inches above the anus. Most people find it easiest to do this in the bathtub. Put a towel in the bottom of the tub for cushioning and lie on your left side. Lubricate the nozzle before insertion. Once the nozzle is inserted, release the water using the clamp on the hose. Go as slowly as you want and stop the flow if you feel a cramp. It will pass. When you feel full – which might be after a few ounces or a whole quart – remove the nozzle. Carefully get out of the tub and sit on the toilet until you've released all the waste water. For anal sex, you will want to repeat this process until the water comes out clear. Be sure to drink some fluids afterwards.

---

Like enemas, douches are sometimes used before sex for hygiene. The vagina is a self-cleaning organ, producing a small amount of normal fluid daily. (This is the regular clear discharge you find on your panties.) In general, douches do more harm than good, as they change the natural pH of the vagina and can make some women more susceptible to yeast infections. They also flush out vaginal lubrication which is vital for comfortable intercourse. However, some women use a cleansing douche toward the end of their periods to flush away any remaining menstrual blood. If you do douche, be sure to use the appropriate nozzle (it has a series of small holes on the sides and is flared), warm water, a very small amount of white vinegar if desired, and gentle pressure. You can squat in the tub or shower or hang the bag near the toilet. Insert the nozzle a few inches into your vagina and release the water flow.

*Suggested Reading: Intimate Invasions* by M.R. Strict offers many hints to increase the safety and eroticism of enema play, as well as several enema-related erotic fantasies.

*Safety Warnings:* Avoid commercial solutions with added fragrances, as many women are violently allergic to them. If you notice any unusual discharge, see your doctor, as this may be a sign of infection.

# Lesson 23. Sexual stamina: controlling orgasm

As a slave, you have given control of yourself to another person. This includes the use of your sexual drives. Many dominants enjoy dictating when and how a slave may orgasm, so it is to your benefit to become aware of your own patterns of sexual response and to learn to direct them.

To this end, Miss Abernathy suggests several exercises to strengthen your pelvic muscles and to control the flow of sexual energy during arousal. You will obtain the best results if you undertake these exercises as regular, daily practices. Neither is complex, but both – particularly together – can have an enormous impact on your sexual self-control.

The first exercise is designed to strengthen the pubococcygeus or PC muscle. The PC muscle is located in the pelvis and supports the genitals, urethra, and anus. The PC muscle controls the flow of urine, so when you are next urinating, try to stop the flow. By doing so, you're contracting your PC muscle. This is also the muscle that contracts rhythmically during orgasm. Like any other muscle, the PC muscle needs regular exercise to function well.

*Activity:* Squeeze your PC muscle tight and then release. Try ten quick contractions (count one one thousand and release) followed by ten longer contractions (three to ten seconds). These contractions – often called "Kegels" after the doctor who discovered the importance of the PC muscle for sexual health – should be done several times a day. Kegels are unnoticeable to others, so you can practice them at any time and in any place.

In addition to physically strengthening your sexual organs, to control orgasm you need to control your sexual response. The following exercise is derived from Tantra, a spiritual path that incorporates meditation and ritualized sex to help the practitioners achieve a blissful state.

Tantra teaches that what we normally identify as orgasm – the explosive pleasure of genital contractions and, in men, ejaculation – is only one step on the ladder of sexual pleasure, and a relatively low step at that. By using our breath, we can move sexual energy from its usual seat in the pelvic region up along energy channels in the body until it floods our heart and brain centers. Tantra practitioners claim that this flow of energy to the brain causes a change in brain function that leads to ecstatic states. This energy can also be directed to various organs in the body for healing and pleasure. The practice introduced here will help you transform "explosive" orgasms to "implosive" ones (as

Tantrika Margo Anand calls them) which, with practice, will help you prolong the sex act as long as you like.

---

*Activity:* Find a time when you can be alone and undisturbed for at least an hour. Recline on a bed or some other comfortable place; you may want a pillow under your head or hips. Begin by taking ten long, deep breaths. As you do so, become aware of how your breath moves from your nose down into your lungs. Feel the way your belly rises with the incoming breath and falls again as you exhale. Continue to breathe deeply from your diaphragm.

Using warm massage oil or your favorite lubricant, begin to massage your genitals until you feel aroused. Continue to stimulate yourself as you become aware of the sexual energy building in your pelvic region. You may sense a tightness or fullness. Now, gently massage your perineum, the area just in front of the anus. Take a deep breath and draw the sexual energy from your pelvis into the perineum. (You might imagine the energy as a pool of light or sense it as warmth – whatever image works best for you is the right one.) As you continue to masturbate, take another deep breath and imagine the energy traveling up your spine and pooling at a spot on the spine behind your navel. With the next breath, the energy will move up to the base of your neck. Another breath with take the energy to the crown of your head. Now breathe again as the energy spills over your forehead, pooling between your eyes. The next breath brings the energy down into your chest and the heart region. Pause here and let the energy collect, then release it back into your lower belly.

As you continue to stimulate yourself, follow the energy path through your body: from the perineum, up the spine to the head, down the front of your body to the heart and the belly and over your genitals back down to the perineum.

Now, when you find yourself approaching orgasm, stop the stimulation, but breathe even more deeply and slowly and allow the energy to keep flowing. Relax your muscles and release any tension. Then begin to stimulate yourself again. Finally, you may approach orgasm and feel that you are being pushed "over the top": as best you can, stop the stimulation and breathe deeply, consciously moving the orgasmic energy along the pathway to your head. You will experience a very different type of orgasm. Instead of a deep throbbing or contractions focused in your genital area, you'll feel a rush of energy in your head and chest. Best of all, this rush will not subside after fifteen or even thirty seconds, but with practice can be sustained for minutes at a time. (Adepts talk of four-hour orgasms.)

Men may notice that they do not ejaculate when they have this type of orgasm, and so they can maintain their erections for much longer. Both men and women will find that instead of feeling exhausted and sleepy after orgasm, they feel energized yet relaxed.

If while practicing this exercise you have a "normal" orgasm, enjoy it and don't indulge in self-criticism. Tantric practitioners spend years learning these techniques. Take up the exercise again another day.

The benefit of this exercise for slaves is the ability, over time, to delay "explosive" orgasms indefinitely, while still enjoying pleasurable (and healthful) feelings. You will ultimately find that you can access sexual energy without direct genital stimulation and can experience some of the same sensations even when you have been forbidden to touch yourself.

> *Suggested Reading: The Art of Sexual Ecstasy* by Margo Anand introduces Tantric techniques in accessible language and with great sensitivity. *Urban Tantra* by Barbara Carrellas updates the traditional practice for modern lovers of all genders and orientations. *Radical Ecstasy* by Dossie Easton and Janet W. Hardy extends these techniques into a BDSM setting.

> *Suggested Viewing: Ancient Secrets of Sexual Ecstasy for Modern Lovers* (heterosexual focus) and *The Art of Extending Orgasm* (heterosexual and lesbian couples) both teach Tantric exercises.

# Lesson 24. Sexual service I: masturbation and erotic touch

Many dominants are unabashed voyeurs. Part of the thrill of control is watching a submissive carry out a task. And that includes sex. Slaves are often called upon to "perform" for a dominant by stripping or masturbating.

---

> *Activity:* Find a time and place where you won't be disturbed. Dress up in your sexiest outfit and put on some erotic music. Lower the lights, if it makes you feel good. Allow yourself to move sensuously to the music. Run your hands over your body. Slowly remove your clothes, garment by garment. When you are naked, begin to masturbate. Stretch out on the floor or the bed and let yourself go.

---

Try this exercise several times or until you are comfortable with it. (Experiment with different outfits and music.) Then, try stripping in front of a full-length mirror. If you are shy at first, try positioning the mirror so you can't see your own face. Watch yourself masturbate. Notice the way your genitals look; listen to the sounds you make as you become more and more excited. Discover what positions and poses look erotic to you.

---

*Activity:* Visit a strip club (men's or women's). Enjoy the show and notice how the dancers move. Can you use of these moves in your own private "strip show"?

---

*Suggested Reading: Sex for One* by Betty Dodson is a virtual masturbation manifesto. It is an excellent introduction to the fine art of self-loving and also contains good advice for those who are pre-orgasmic. If you feel foolish or frightened of performing, try Carol Queen's *Exhibitionism for the Shy*, a warm and witty guide to awakening your inner exhibitionist. *Men Loving Themselves* by Jack Morin and *I Am My Lover: Women Pleasure Themselves*, ed. Joani Blank, are beautifully photographed studies of men and women masturbating.

*Resources:* The Learning Annex, which has branches in most major American cities, regularly offers personal enrichment courses on "How to Strip for Your Lover."

A good sex slave should know how to pleasure a dominant in as many ways as possible. Among these, erotic touch is the most important, as it plays a role in all the more obvious forms of sex play.

---

*Exercise:* List ten different items (including body parts) with which you could touch someone erotically: feather, long hair, velvet....

---

*Activity:* Collect 6-8 different items from your list above and put them in a box. When you next masturbate, close your eyes (or blindfold yourself) and choose something from the box. Touch your nipples, your belly, your face with it.

*Activity:* Get a professional, non-erotic massage. Notice the different types of touch the massage therapist uses. Which felt good to you? Did you find any of them erotic? You may also want to visit an erotic masseur or masseuse; some sex workers will be happy to teach you skills, particularly if you explain your circumstances. (Please be aware of any laws in your area regarding sex work before undertaking this activity and use your best judgment.)

**Suggested Reading:** *The Complete Illustrated Guide to Massage by* Stewart Mitchell **is an excellent general introduction, and Anne Hooper's** *Massage and Loving* **is good for a more erotic focus.**

**Suggested Viewing.** *The Intimate Guide to Male Genital Massage.* **The movie** *9 1/2 Weeks,* **although profoundly ambivalent about dominance and submission, does contain a few erotically charged scenes involving the sense of touch and food. If you are a pre-orgasmic woman, you'll find** *Becoming Orgasmic* **a reassuring and helpful video. You may also enjoy Betty Dodson's** *Self-Loving.* **For information on using vibrators, watch Carol Queen's** *Great Vibrations.*

# Lesson 25. Clothing, restraint, and chastity d

As a sex slave, you must maintain a constant awareness both of your status as property and of your role as a sex toy. Much BDSM fiction would have us believe that sex slaves do nothing all day but pleasure voluptuous libertines. Even if you are a live-in slave serving more than one dominant, it is very likely you'll have other tasks as well. How can you maintain your submission when you're walking the dog or picking up the dry cleaning? This is a challenge for all slaves, but I mention it here because of all the specialized roles, sex slaves seem to have the most difficulty with it, perhaps because their role is essentially private. House servants may come and go more freely and are likely to deal with a wide variety of people in the course of their daily routines. They may get outside approval for their efficiency or skill. A sex slave's skills are not regularly displayed outside the privacy of the dominant's house.

With this challenge in mind, some dominants choose to outfit their slaves with unobtrusive items of clothing or chastity devices as ways of emphasizing their control and the slave's submission. Most often, the clothing is in the form of undergarments and may have a restraining character, like a corset. It may also have a cross-dressing element, as when a businessman is made to wear stockings and garters under his banker's grays. In this lesson, you'll experiment with such "hidden items."

---

*Activity:* Wear a tight-fitting undergarment today. It should be an item you usually do not wear, and it should not restrict your breathing. (Spandex bicycling shorts or a leotard are good choices.)

At the end of the day, answer these questions: How did wearing this garment change your day? Were you aware of the garment? Did it affect your ability to perform any tasks? Did you find the restriction in any way erotic? What if the garment were a corset, waist-training belt, or (for a man) pantyhose? Do you find that wearing any of these garments makes you feel especially submissive? Are you still able to carry on with your normal activities such as shopping or running errands?

Now, try wearing pantyhose (if you're a man) or a jockstrap (if you're a woman). Is your erotic response different?

## Notes on corsetry

Once a mainstay of a woman's wardrobe, the corset is now firmly in the domain of fetishists and body modification artists. Since it is such a popular item in the BDSM community and figures so greatly into the mythology of sex, I mention it here.

*Activity:* Visit a corsetier and, if possible, try on a corset. (Men may be surprised to hear that many corsetmakers also have designs specifically for them!)

*Suggested Reading:* **Fans of corsetry will enjoy *Support and Seduction: A History of Corsets and Bras* by Beatrice Fontanel, a lushly illustrated coffee table book. The best source of information on waist-training and corsetry with an eye to dominance and submission is *Body Play and Modern Primitives Quarterly,* formerly a print publication published by piercing instructor and body modification artist Fakir Musafar, now online at www.bodyplay.com/bodyplay/index.htm.**

*Suggested Viewing:* **The opening scenes of *Gone with the Wind* see Scarlett being laced into her corset.**

### Chastity Devices

Chastity devices are another way for dominants to assert their erotic control. If you've been working with the Tantric exercises suggested in one of the previous lessons, you will be developing greater control over your sexual energies. Chastity devices can be an exquisite way to increase that control.

The most common chastity device for men is a penis restraint or "cock cage." Usually made of leather or metal, this item is fastened around the penis and testicles and prevents the man from touching his penis, while allowing him to urinate. Chastity "belts" for women usually fasten around the waist or hips and block access to the clitoris and vagina; they also allow the woman to urinate.

---

*Activity:* Visit a sex toy store and select a chastity device. If you will be locking and unlocking it yourself, be sure the lock is easily accessible. Begin by wearing the device for one day only. Build up to several days at a time. Write about your responses in your slave journal.

---

See also the next lesson, on anal plugs.

# Lesson 26. Anal plugs

Review Lesson 22 on Enemas. Anal or "butt" plugs are another common device used to control sexual response and induce a submissive mindset. By increasing the size of the plugs over a period of time, it is also possible to train the body to more easily accommodate larger items and enjoy anal intercourse.

Anal plugs come in a delightful array of shapes and sizes. If you are just beginning to explore anal play, choose a small plug. Silicone toys tend to hold body heat well and are quite resilient.

*Safety Warning:* **Anal plugs should be smooth, with no sharp edges or seams, and should have a flared base.**

They should not be made of any breakable material. Always use a water-soluble lubricant with rubber toys. If you suffer from hemorrhoids, be careful with any kind of anal play, as friction will exacerbate your condition. Use plenty of lubricant and keep a good hemorrhoid medicine on hand. Of the over-the-counter preparations, Anusol seems to work the best.

---

*Activity:* Purchase a good quality anal plug. You may even want to buy one small one and one somewhat larger one "to grow into." Some anal plugs have graduated "bulbs" or "beads" for a one-size-fits-all effect.

Spend some time exploring your anus. You may want to take a warm bath and a gentle enema. Trim your nails and file them down so there are no sharp edges, or wear a latex glove if you have long nails. Warm some lubricant in your hand and massage your anal area, including the perineum, the space just in front of the anus. Circle the wrinkled outer surface of the anus with your finger. Slowly insert your finger. You may also want to stimulate your penis or clitoris. Allow your finger to rest just inside the sphincter. Can you feel your pulse? Experiment to see if you enjoy the sensation of fullness more, or whether you crave movement. When you feel ready, apply lubricant to the plug and begin to insert it very slowly. Stop if you feel any pain. Your sphincter may try to clamp down on the plug. Breathe deeply and relax, while you stimulate your clitoris or penis. When your anus has gotten used to the fullness, continue. Some people find a twisting or screwing motion makes insertion easier.

Don't worry if it takes you several sessions before you can insert the plug all the way. Once you have it in, relax for a while. You may want to masturbate, or just observe the sensations. Try walking around; a properly shaped plug won't come out.

---

As you become more accustomed to anal plugs, you may want to experiment with wearing them for longer periods of time. This can be rewarding, but be sure to allow yourself to have bowel movements as necessary.

> **Suggested Reading: *Anal Pleasure and Health* by Jack Morin has become something of a classic in the field. It will provide you with basic information on anatomy and safety. Also consider Tristan Taormino's *Ultimate Guide to Anal Sex for Women* and Bill Brent's *Ultimate Guide to Anal Sex for Men.***

> *Suggested Viewing: Self Anal Massage for Men.*

# Lesson 27. Sexual service II: oral service

Not all that long ago, oral sex was considered wild, a sexual taboo. (Frighteningly enough, it is technically illegal in some American states even today, falling under the rubric of "sodomy.") Still, the sexual revolution made oral lovemaking an acceptable and expected part of the erotic repertoire. And judging from the reports of dominatrices and phone sex workers, providing oral service to a dominant is one of the most common submissive fantasies.

Why? Because oral sex is focused on the pleasure of the receiver, not the giver. Although s/he may derive some gratification and pleasure from the act, the slave serving a dominant orally must postpone his or her own orgasm, perhaps indefinitely. The dominant remains the center of attention and pleasure.

---

*Activity:* Buy a selection ot ripe fruit, including, if possible, strawberries, peaches, bananas, and mangoes, as well as some whipping cream. Wash and peel the fruits as needed and arrange them attractively in a bowl. Whip the cream with a little sugar until it peaks. Now repair to the bedroom.

Take off your clothes and have a towel handy. Begin by taking a piece of fruit and dipping it into the cream. Notice the beautiful contrast of the deep red of the berries or the vibrant yellow-orange of the mango and the pale white of the cream. Run your tongue along the fruit, licking off the cream. Note the texture of the fruit, its scent, its rich juices. Put the fruit in your mouth and feel the cream melt against your tongue. Linger over the subtle flavors.

Adorn your naked body with fruit. Use the banana to paint your nipples and belly with cream, then lick the banana clean. Decorate yourself with berries. Let your now sticky-sweet finger trail between your legs, along your thighs. Stroke your genitals. As you pleasure yourself, enjoy the taste of the fruit as it mingles with your own flavors. Focus on the softness of your mouth and the sweetness of the fruit. As you climax, pay attention to your tongue and lips: are they more sensitive? (Feel free to share this activity with a friend, too.)

Now, taste your own sexual fluids. Are they salty? Sweet? Pungent?

---

*Activity:* Along with oral sex, slaves are often called upon to perform other kinds of oral service. For this activity you will need a leather shoe or boot. Kneel down and put your hand inside the shoe with your fingers in the toe area. Now make love to the shoe with your mouth. As you do so, pay attention to the sensations your hand feels. How much pressure should you apply? How much is too much? Rub your cheek against the side of the shoe – can you feel it inside? Experiment with different kinds of footwear: thick engineer boots require a very different oral touch from fine leather pumps.

---

*Activity:* Practice flicking your tongue over and around the tip of your forefinger. Make circles as well as up-and-down and side-to-side motions.

---

*Activity:* Use a lifelike dildo to practice your technique.

---

By building up the sensitivity of your lips and tongue, you are preparing yourself to give more subtle oral service. If you don't have someone on whom to practice your technique, please watch the video listed in "*Suggested Viewing*" carefully.

**Suggested Reading:** Violet Blue's *Ultimate Guide to Cunnilingus* and *Ultimate Guide to Fellatio.*

**Suggested Viewing:** *Nina Hartley's Guide to Oral Sex.* Porn star and registered nurse Nina Hartley gives a caring and joyful introduction to fellatio and cunnilingus in this video. Highly recommended.

**Safety Warning:** There is no consensus within the medical community about whether HIV, the virus believed to cause AIDS, can be transmitted during unprotected oral sex. However, we do know that other STDs, such as herpes, are transmitted by oral-genital contact. The best way to avoid all of those diseases — barring abstinence — is to use a latex barrier (condom or dental dam) during oral sex.

# Lesson 28. Sexual service III: vaginal

In addition to serving a dominant woman with your mouth, you may be called upon to pleasure her vaginally. The important point to keep in mind here is that the dominant's sexual pleasure is always primary. Of course, this is also the case if you are a female slave who is required to make her body available for use by a dominant.

---

*Exercise:* List at least five ways that you could pleasure a woman vaginally without a penis.

---

## Sex Toys: Dildos and Vibrators

Although dildos are depicted in ancient art and are among the oldest sexual artifacts we possess, they maintain a certain mystique. Vibrators are a much more recent invention, of course, and were first used not as "sports massagers" but to treat "hysteria" in female patients. Apparently doctors discovered that a good orgasm or twelve went a long way toward relieving the stresses of Victorian life.

If you are honored with the opportunity to pleasure a dominant woman with a dildo or vibrator, try to think of the toy as an extension of yourself. The dominant will undoubtedly direct you, but imagine the dildo as part of your sex or hand; think of the vibrator as your ideal tongue.

---

*Activity:* Visit a sex toy store and learn about the variety of products on the market. (If visiting a store is not an option in your area, please study the *Suggested*

*Reading* volume carefully.) What are the advantages of a battery-operated vibrator? The disadvantages? What kind of lubricants are compatible with silicone dildos? Which dildos can be used with a harness?

*Suggested Reading: The Good Vibrations Guide to Sex* by **Cathy Winks and Anne Semans gives a good overview of the different types of sex toys available.**

*Suggested Viewing:* **For information on using vibrators, watch Carol Queen's *Great Vibrations*.**

---

*Activity:* If you don't already own one, purchase a vibrator. Use it when you masturbate to get a sense of its advantages. (Male slaves can also enjoy vibrators!)

---

**The penis as sex toy**

Some male slaves report that they find it difficult to maintain a submissive attitude when asked to pleasure a dominant woman sexually. Since some people feel that sex is inherently degrading, especially for women, these men may feel that they must become "aggressive" when they have intercourse with a woman. Even when their submission is utterly sincere, it may be a challenge to overcome this false programming.

Remember that the dominant's pleasure is primary; your role is to facilitate and augment her enjoyment of the act. Your penis belongs to her just as fully as the rest of you. It is her toy. Practice the Tantric exercise given earlier in this section as a way of controlling your own orgasm.

---

*Activity:* Use a penis restraint (cock ring or cock cage) as a reminder to yourself that your penis is for Mistress's pleasure.

---

*Activity:* If you have difficulty controlling your orgasm, create a cassette tape to use during masturbation. Choose a phrase that expresses your submission ("Mistress's pleasure is my reward," for example) and record your voice saying it slowly and clearly. If you find that you normally orgasm after five minutes, record the phrase for six minutes, followed by the command: "Come now!" Then repeat the process, allowing an additional minute each time.

This exercise will teach you to control your sexual response by associating it with a certain phrase. Then, when you are called upon to pleasure your Mistress, repeat the phrase silently in your head.

*Safety Warning:* **With all the (justifiable) concern these days with disease prevention, Miss Abernathy finds it important to remind you of another delicate matter: pregnancy. If you are engaging in activities that might lead to pregnancy and do not wish to parent a child, please use an appropriate contraceptive.**

## Vaginal fisting

Miss Abernathy must admit that in matters of fisting, a picture really is worth a thousand words. Luckily, there exists a fine book that has both in abundance. If you are new to fisting, please read the volume listed in the *Suggested Reading* section of this lesson before proceeding.

"Fisting," a rather unfortunate term for this delicate art, is simply inserting one's whole hand into a woman's open and willing vagina. It requires sensitivity, good communication, and copious quantities of lubricant. Feeling a woman's body open to receive your hand is a quite incomparable experience, both awe-inspiring and humbling, and a slave who is offered an opportunity to experience it should feel honored.

Some people discover fisting quite by accident. A lover has inserted a finger or two, and as the woman becomes more excited, she asks for "More, more!" After four fingers, the only option is to tuck the thumb under and push slowly until the muscles at the mouth of the vagina open sufficiently to allow your hand entry. For some women, only the slightest movement of the hand will induce orgasms by the dozen; others prefer a gentle in-and-out or twisting motion. Some enjoy a vigorous romp on your hand. In all cases, large amounts of lubricant are in order. (Avoid lubricants that contain nonoxynol-9, as it appears many women are violently allergic to it.) The use of latex (or, for the latex-sensitive, nitrile) gloves for this activity is also recommended, first for reasons of safer sex, but also because it seems to decrease the chance of urinary tract infections. Women who enjoy being fisted will benefit from drinking extra fluids and taking cranberry extract tablets (available at health food stores) il they are prone to urinary irritation.

If you are a female slave whose Owner enjoys fisting you, there are ways you can train your body to be more receptive.

---

*Activity:* Obtain a number of dildos of varying sizes. You may also want to include some larger anal plugs. Using lubricant, insert a dildo that is a comfortable fit and masturbate for a while. If you feel your vaginal muscles clenching the dildo, consciously relax them. As you become more excited, your vagina will open and become more elastic. Try inserting progressively larger dildos over a period of time. Please note that your menstrual cycle may well affect your comfort level with this exercise. Be aware of changes in your body and do not force anything.

---

*Suggested Reading: A Hand in the Bush: The Fine Art of Vaginal Fisting* by Deborah Addington is the only book-length introduction to this delightful practice.

## G-spot stimulation

One of the many advantages of fisting and other manual play is that it allows for easy stimulation of the G-spot, the spongy area on the front wall of the vagina that responds, in some women, very positively to massage. (The G-spot has been compared to the male prostate gland in terms of erotic sensation.) Stimulating the G-spot seems in turn to stimulate the portion of the clitoris that is internal, and for some women, induces a very deep, intense orgasm. Orgasm may be accompanied by "female ejaculation," a spray of clear liquid from within the vagina. (In the past, some people have taken this liquid to be urine, although recent studies indicate that it is akin to seminal fluid.)

Women with active G-spots may enjoy massage with fingers, vibrators, or dildos. Sexual positions that allow a penis or dildo to ride "high," rubbing against the front wall of the vagina, can also stimulate the area. (These positions may also irritate the urethra, so women who are troubled with urinary tract infections may want to try other methods of G-spot stimulation.)

*Suggested Viewing: The Complete Guide to Sexual Positions* demonstrates one hundred different positions for heterosexual couples, many of which can be adapted for female partners who enjoy dildo play. *How to Female Ejaculate* (various orientations) and *Incredible G-Spot* (heterosexual focus) include techniques for G-spot stimulation. *Private Pleasures and Shadows*, a lesbian-made video, contains a beautiful vaginal fisting scene.

# Lesson 29. Sexual service IV: anal

If you've tried the exercises suggested in the lessons on enemas and anal plugs, you will already have learned quite a bit about your body and its responses to anal stimulation. If you are called upon to be the receptive partner in anal sex, you will need to do two things: relax and communicate. Working with anal plugs will have taught you how to relax the sphincter; breathe deeply and push out. (Pushing out may seem countermtuitive, but it opens the sphincter.)

Communication is a more subtle issue. If you experience any pain, you must immediately tell the dominant, but you should do so in a way that is both respectful and direct: Mistress! The dildo is at a painful angle, Mistress! or Master! May I have more lube, please, Master? Anal tissue is very delicate, and it is sometimes hard for the active partner to gauge your needs from body cues alone.

Likewise, if after being used anally you notice any bleeding or other problems, inform the dominant immediately! It isn't unusual for small tears to cause slight bleeding – this can also occur after a hard, dry bowel movement, you'll notice – but it is the dominant's responsibility to care for you, so do not withhold this sort of information in an attempt at delicacy or humility.

If you are required to be the active partner in anal service, you should remember three keys to successful anal play:

1)      Go slowly.

2)      Use at least twice as much lubricant as you think you need.

3)      Communicate.

Again, communication should be direct but respectful, especially since many people find the extreme intimacy of anal penetration makes them feel vulnerable. Describe your actions just before you do them:

Master, I'm entering you slowly now, Master. (Note that some dominants will prefer you to refer to your penis as "theirs" to remind you that your body is their property: Master, I'm putting your cock inside you now, Master.) If you are using a dildo for penetration, you will need to communicate all the more, as you won't be able to feel resistance as readily.

If you think you may be called upon to service a dominant anally, be sure to read at least one of the titles suggested below and review safer sex procedures for anal sex.

> *Suggested Reading:* **Most general sex manuals will cover anal sex, but rarely in great detail. In addition to the titles mentioned in the lesson on anal plugs, you may enjoy** *Bert Herman's Trust: The Hand Book.*

> *Suggested Viewing: Nina Hartley's Guide to Anal Sex.*

# Body Servants: Ladies' Maids and Valets

Body servants are those responsible primarily for the physical care of their Owners. These are traditional roles, once considered among the most respectable and trusted positions in service. Because body servants work closely with their Owners, often in intimate settings like the bath or dressing room, they often enjoy the privileged role of confidant(e). These roles are also favorite subjects for BDSM erotica, as the personal nature of the lady's maid or valet suggests the possibility of sexual intimacy as well.

In modern household settings; where the number of servants is generally limited, the maid or valet may also perform services usually associated with the personal assistant or housekeeper or escort. In particular, the valet may double as a butler.

## Lesson 30. Basic personal attendance

Review: Lessons on Obedience, Personal Care, and Positioning the Body. In these earlier lessons, you learned to take stock of your surroundings and to be aware of other people's presence and emotions. These are vitally important skills for all types of personal servants. You must learn to focus your attention on your Owner and to respond to his or her needs, even those that may remain unspoken.

The most fundamental type of service a maid* provides is what I refer to as fetch-and-carry. S/he will be expected to respond primarily to verbal commands (often answering verbally as well) by fetching items and conveying them to the Owner in a variety of postures. Of course, grace is paramount here. If the maid is slow or clumsy, s/he will not please.

*Activity:* To improve your posture, practice walking with a book balanced on your head. (If you plan to wear high heels for service, practice with them on.)

When you feel comfortable with this exercise, try crawling with a large book balanced on your back. (If you have knee or back problems that could be exacerbated by this posture, skip this activity.)

*Activity:* Procure a large tray (silver is lovely, but heavy). Practice carrying the tray – empty at first – and setting it down on a table until you can do so gracefully and with a minimum of noise. Then try carrying empty cups and saucers or glasses. Finally, fill the cups or glasses with water. Can you hold a laden tray with one hand while you distribute cups or glasses? (This will depend on the size and the weight of the tray, so do not be discouraged if you cannot manage with a full tray. The point is to know what you can and cannot handle.) Remember when lifting a heavy object to bend at the knees, not the waist, to avoid back strain; this is especially important if you are wearing heels.

---

* For simplicity's sake, I refer throughout this section to maids. The maid's role is one of the most popular in D/S arrangements, for both men and women, and so I have preferred the term here. I extend my apologies to the valets among my readers, a rarer but no less noble breed.

*Activity:* Visit a busy restaurant and notice how the servers and busboys handle plates. Practice some of these techniques at home.

*Activity:* Practice picking up and carrying small objects with your mouth. Try to avoid salivating on the object.

*Activity:* The curtsey is a very pretty skill for maids. To begin, stand erect. Step back with your right foot and bend down – your right knee will move toward your left foot. As you lower yourself, move your arms out to your sides. Keep your back straight and your head up. When you've bent as far as you can, bow your head gracefully for a heartbeat, then rise. Practice until you can perform the curtsey with fluid grace. In general, a full curtsey is reserved for when one is in evening wear (e.g. a floor-length skirt), so practice a shallower "bob" too.

The masculine equivalent is the bow. Bend forward from the hips approximately 20-45 degrees and nod your head slightly. Pause and rise. A shallower bow (from the waist) is less formal, but quicker and more practical for many occasions.

A helpful hint: Personal attendance is made much easier by excellent household organization. If you've made yourself familiar with the contents of the house, when Mistress asks you to fetch that old playbill from nineteen-ought-three, you'll know where to find it.

*Further Training:* See the lesson for butlers for information on more advanced table service and the cooking chapter in the Household Management section for guides to tea service.

*Suggested Reading: A Modern Man's Guide to Life*, pp. 329-332. This section will provide a useful review of etiquette for maids and valets alike. For a slave, the hints are applicable regardless of the gender of the person you serve.

*Suggested Viewing:* The film *Dangerous Liaisons* – in particular the opening scenes – for a glimpse of the historical roles of man- and maid-servants.

*Resources:* Since balance is important to a maid, consider enrolling in ballet or yoga classes. Activities that build arm strength are also helpfuL

# Lesson 31. Voice-training III: verbal response

An attractive speaking voice is a great asset in a maid. While sex slaves, for example, may only need the most basic voice-training skills, maids are often called upon to express opinions and may also need to engage in polite conversation from time to time. These skills become all the more important if the maid is undertaking other responsibilities, such as business affairs (personal assistant) or social outings (escort). This lesson will provide you with exercises to help improve your speech.

---

*Activity:* Record yourself having a conversation (set the recorder by the telephone, for example), or ask a friend to do so. (You may have to let the tape run for a while before you relax enough to speak naturally.)

Now, listen to the tape. Identify any verbal "tics" you may have. These may be meaningless filler phrases like "um" or "you know" or "like," or they may be habits like clearing your throat before speaking or laughing to distract from the harshness of a pointed statement.

---

It can be difficult to correct such habits, but it can be done. Try speaking more slowly. Before you open your mouth, mentally count to three and take a deep breath. Try to arrange your thoughts before you begin, as many tics are stalling devices to aid in "thinking on your feet." Ask a trusted friend to monitor your progress.

> *Resources:* If you find this task overwhelming on your own, consider hiring a voice coach. These professionals often have a background in theater or speech pathology and can help you improve both the tone of your voice and your diction. They can sometimes help you modify a regional accent, too. General assertiveness training usually contains a voice coaching component as well.

# Lesson 32. Uniforms for maids

While all types of slaves may wear uniforms, it is the maid who is most closely identified with a particular style of dress: a short black dress with a frilly white apron and a small white cap. Fetish versions of this "French maid" outfit may include crinolines, seamed stockings, and high-heeled shoes and are readily available from lingerie shops like Frederick's of Hollywood.

What you wear when serving is primarily a matter of the Owner's taste and budget and your assigned tasks. Your uniform will be chosen to express your role and, to an extent, your personality. Ideally, you need an outfit that is proper but practical. Fetishwear, while lovely, should be reserved for special occasions – parties, teas, and the like – or for the bedroom. In all cases, uniforms should be clean and in good repair. The following exercises will help you determine your own needs and preferences in day-to-day uniforms.

*Activity:* Visit a hotel or other location where you will see professional maids at work. What tasks are they performing? What kinds of movements do they make: crouching, bending, reaching...? What kind of uniform, if any, do they wear?

*Activity:* Visit a uniform supply store that carries a line for domestic servants. (Check the Yellow Pages for listings.) If no such store is available in your area, search out mail order houses or call a local professional maid service and ask where they get their uniforms. Given the tasks you expect to perform, what style of uniform would be most suitable?

Perhaps the most important reason for servants to wear a uniform is that it sets them apart for special tasks and also serves to remind them of their role. Even if a formal maid's uniform is beyond your means, you can use other items to help remind you of your submission.

*Activity:* Select an item such as a piece of jewelry or an article of clothing that reminds you of your status as a slave-in-training. Put this item on whenever you perform service tasks, even something as simple as writing in your slave journal or studying this book. Record your reactions. Now try wearing this item every day for a week. Does your perception of it change? Do you feel "submissive" all the time? Does it shift your awareness to your slavehood? How?

*Resources:* **The House of Uniforms (852 Lexington Ave. between 64th and 65th Sts., New York, 1-888-707-3746, www.HouseofUniforms.com) carries a wide** selection of classic and modern apparel for maids and housekeepers. They ship world-wide. This is not a fetish boutique, so please be discreet in your inquiries.

# Lesson 33. Cross-dressing

The "sissy maid" – a cross-dressed male in service to a female – is a staple of BDSM erotica. It is a role favored both by fetishistic crossdressers, who derive erotic gratification from being dressed in the clothing of another gender, and by some seeking a safe way of exploring and expressing their inner feminine selves. Women, too, may derive pleasure and satisfaction from wearing men's clothing and serving as a valet or butler.

If cross-dressing interests you, it is important to ascertain the source of your attraction to it. As I indicated above, cross-dressers usually fall into one of several categories:

- fetishists or erotic cross-dressers;
- those who experience cross-dressing as humiliating;
- transformational cross-dressers.

If you are a fetishist, your primary interest in cross-dressing is erotic. You regularly find yourself sexually aroused when dressed, often by the feel of certain fabrics, like silk or velvet. Dressing may be part of your masturbation rituals. You don't necessarily feel less masculine (or feminine) when dressed.

Perhaps you find cross-dressing humiliating. If you are a butch woman who was forced to wear traditionally feminine clothing or an effeminate man who was made to act "like a real man" at some point in your life, you want to play out scenes that involve "forced" cross-dressing. The satisfaction you derive would come from experiencing feelings of shame about your dress. You may fantasize about being verbally humiliated about your appearance. You may also connect these feelings with submission or with sexual arousal.

If you are most interested in exploring the feminine (or masculine) components of your personality – in Jungian terms, your anima or animus – you may want to experiment with transformational cross-dressing. Here you dress to "pass" as another gender, masking those aspects of your appearance and behavior that express your usual gender presentation. You may be exploring your gender identity, or you may identify as transgendered.

While it is certainly possible to integrate any of these scenarios into your submission, they all pose certain challenges. If you are a fetishist, you may find it difficult to serve as a maid without the promise of some sexual play. You may want to consider training primarily as a sex slave, or including specific sexual techniques in your maid training. If you are determined to make domestic service and cross-dressing parts of your life, you must learn to control your sexual responses while dressed so that you can concentrate on your work.

If you enjoy humiliation, it may be very difficult for you to focus on work at all while dressed, as your emotions may run very high. You may also require a great deal of attention from the dominant in order to derive satisfaction from your experience. I would suggest that if you are capable of submission without dressing, you save dressing for special erotic "mind games" with the dominant, separate from day-to-day service.\*

If you are a transformational cross-dresser, it is very possible to integrate your alternate persona into your maid service. Quite simply, while in service, you appear, and are treated as, the gender you wish to present. You will need to schedule your time carefully,

---

\* *If you only feel submissive when dressed, but feel a need to be humiliated for this, I suggest that your needs might better be met by carefully constructed short-term BDSM scenes than in full-time service. Slavehood requires that you be able to put aside your immediate desires, including those for attention, positive or negative. Whatever the case, please spend some time exploring your overall feelings about submission before proceeding.*

since transformational cross-dressing can be a time-consuming activity, and you want to have sufficient time to accomplish your service tasks as well.

If you want to experiment with cross-dressing, try the following exercise.

*Activity:* Buy a pair of underpants of a type usually worn by another gender. These may be bikinis, briefs, or thongs for male slaves, or boxers, jock straps or briefs for women. Choose a fabric and style that you find pleasing. Wear the underpants under your regular street clothes. Record your feelings in your slave journal.

If you find you enjoy this exercise, you can expand it by wearing other garments – men's dress shirts and trousers or women's skirts and blouses. You may want to experiment with makeup or a false mustache. Write about your experiences and share them with your trainer.

*Suggested Reading: Miss Vera's Finishing School for Boys Who Want to Be Girls* by Veronica Vera is a delightful must-read by the founder of the world's first cross-dressing academy. Miss Vera, herself a wonder to behold, will guide you step-by-step through the process of transformational cross-dressing. (See also Resources for more information on her school.) Charles Anders's *The Lazy Crossdresser* offers extraordinarily helpful hints and ideas for the non-transformational cross-dresser. *Information for the Female to Male Cross Dresser and Transsexual* by Lou Sullivan provides helpful hints of use to female valets. See especially pp. 35-51.

*Resources:* If you are a male lady's maid, you might consider treating yourself to a few days in the able hands of Miss Veronica Vera. Visit www.missvera.com or call 888-386-8372 for a brochure and application.

# Lesson 34. Attending a lady: the maid

Among the most popular roles for submissives is the lady's maid. Ladies' maids may be of any gender, as, indeed, may be the ladies they serve. (The male "sissy maid" is a perennial favorite.) The maid role also has a devoted following among submissive fetishists, since it allows them to deal extensively with Mistress's wardrobe, and perhaps to wear a fetish-style uniform as well (see "Uniforms" above).

Traditionally, the realm of the maid was the bedroom and dressing room, where s/he was expected to help Madame with her toilette – clothing, makeup, and hair. S/he might also help in the bath. (BDSM erotica often moves the maid into the parlor to serve tea.) A maid would also accompany the Mistress wherever she traveled and might attend her while shopping. (Butlers might also be expected to perform these tasks.) Unlike some other slaves who appear in public – personal secretaries and escorts, for example – maids generally wear a uniform that sets them apart.

As a maid, you should learn as much as you can about a lady's toilette, both in theory and in practice. If you are working independently, you may choose to "serve yourself" for the time being.

## Clothing

*Activity:* Inventory a wardrobe (your own or your trainer's). Make a comprehensive list of all the items of clothing, from underwear to outerwear. List colors, sizes, and types of fabric along with the style of garment: powder blue cashmere sweater set, size medium; 18 pairs black silk panties, size small. If you send clothing out to be laundered, this is an excellent opportunity to mark garments with a permanent laundry marker or to sew in name labels. (Use initials and be sure to wtite where the ink will not be visible when the garment is being worn.) You may also want to weed out items that are no longer being worn for storage, sale, or to give away. Note also which items seem to be "old standbys" as these will give you the best sense of a person's preferred style.

---

*Activity:* Organize the wardrobe. You may want to see about adding an extra bar in the closet or buying some shelves for sweaters. Group the clothing by use (casual, formal, sport) and then by length, separating short sleeves from long sleeves, and perhaps, light colors from dark. Try to store any accessories, like scarves, with the garments they match: hang scarves on the hanger with dresses and blouses.

Now organize any shoes. If there are some that are worn only infrequently, store them in boxes, and tape a Polaroid picture of the pair to the end of the box for easy identification.

---

*Activity:* Practice setting out complete outfits, including jewelry (necklaces and bracelets can be hung over the hanger). Are there new combinations you might not have tried before?

---

It is important to get a sense of your Owner's style, particularly if you will be attending her as she shops. She may ask you for suggestions or opinions on garments, and if you are aware of her tastes, you will be in a better position to advise her. Familiarize yourself with her favorite shops. Does she read any fashion magazines? What public figures does she admire? Notice when she comments on another woman's dress: what does she find attractive? Tacky? If you are working independently, try to determine what your own taste says about you. Are you a classic dresser? Sporty? Provocative?

> *Suggested Reading: Work Clothes: Casual Dress for Serious Work* by Kim Johnson Gross, et al. covers men's and women's attire. *Lucy's List* by Lucy D. Curtis contains shopping tips for women who wear larger sizes. Elsa Klensch's *Style* is a basic guide to women's fashions and accessories.

## Makeup and Hair

In addition to clothing, maids must be familiar with skin care and makeup. If you are a woman yourself, you may already be comfortable with makeup techniques. Review your own responses to the "Personal Care for Slaves" lesson to get a sense of how you relate to "beauty culture."

---

*Activity:* Take a class in makeup and skin care. Local beauty colleges and department stores often offer "makeover" classes.

---

*Activity:* Get a makeover at a cosmetic counter or visit a spa for a facial. Notice both what tools the aesthetician uses and her way of touching the skin.

---

*Activity:* Make a point of reading some of the more popular fashion and beauty magazines to get a sense of both classic makeup techniques and the current styles. *Elle* and *Vogue* have regular makeup columns and *Allure* is devoted to personal care alone (as opposed to fashion).

---

Finally, some maids are asked to style their Mistress's hair. While some styles require a good deal of skill, others need only a little practice. Again, fashion and beauty magazines are a good source of information and ideas.

> *Suggested Reading: Making Faces* by Keith Aucoin, *Women's Face: Skin Care and Makeup* by Kim Johnson Gross, et al., *Ultimate Makeup & Beauty* by Mary Quant, *Hair: A Book of Braiding and Styles* by Anne Akers Johnson, *Haircutting at Home* by John R. Albano.

# Lesson 35. Attending a gentleman: the valet

The valet (traditionally pronounced in English with the emphasis on the first syllable and a hard "t" at the end) is the masculine equivalent of the lady's maid. Also called a manservant, "gentleman's gentleman" or simply so–and–so's "man," the valet assists in a gentleman's toilette and may often fulfill other functions, such as light cleaning and cooking, correspondence and errands, or driving. He may also escort a gentleman on his travels.

## Clothing

In general, a man's toilette is much simpler than a woman's. Aside from simple matters of grooming, many of which will be taken care of by the man's barber, men need only make sure that they and their clothing are clean and tidy. It is the valet's job to assure that all clothing is properly looked after and, often, to assemble outfits for the gentleman to don.

> *Activity:* See the Clothing Inventory exercise in Lesson 31.

Men's fashion, particularly in business and formal dress, changes much more slowly and subtly than women's. Barring any radical changes in his size, a man can expect to wear a conservative, well-constructed suit for years, not just a season or two. Also the difference in quality between a well-made suit and a shoddy one is vast, whereas women are often shocked to discover that expensive designer clothes hold up no better than their mid-range counterparts. Since a decent suit will set a gentleman back at least $500, valets are most often charged with caring for suits and other expensive garments. A valet-in-training will need to learn as much as possible about men's clothing.

*Activity:* Visit an upscale clothier. Examine – and, if possible, try on – some well-made suits. (See the *Suggested Reading* for tips on how to distinguish a good suit from one that is merely expensive.) Engage the salesperson in conversation about the differences between styles and brands of suits.

Most suits require dry cleaning – the well-dressed man shuns "wash and wear" suits – but the cleaning process can quickly weaken the fabric's fibers and age the suit prematurely. Instead, brush the suit and steam out any wrinkles. Suits should only be cleaned when they have visible stains or if airing does not remove the smell of tobacco or body odors.

*Activity:* Learn how to brush and steam a suit. You will also want to learn how to iron a dress shirt. (You can ask your tailor for help, or read one of the books listed here.)

*Suggested Reading: Clothes and the Man: the Principles of Fine Men's Dress* and *Style and the Man* by **Alan Flusser** are the two best introductions to the fine art of dressing a man well. *Paisley Goes with Nothing* by **Hal Rubenstein** with **Jim Mullen**, a more recent title, provides humorous but sound advice on matters of style as well as the social graces. *Work Clothes: Casual Dress for Serious Work* by Kim Johnson Gross, et al, covers men's and women's attire for "casual Fridays" and beyond. *Color for Men* by Carole Jackson with Kalia Lulow applies the four-season color principles to men's dress.

### Leather care: shoes, boots, and accessories

Dress shoes and boots often rival suits for the position of most expensive item in a man's wardrobe, and like suits, leather shoes are expected to last for years with proper care. Studies have shown that in a traditional business environment, mussed hair and even a threadbare jacket can be overlooked, but down-at-the-heels shoes make a singularly bad impression. The solution: regular polishing.

Valets with a military background will have a distinct advantage here, but it is important to remember that fine, thin leather should be treated with more care than the thicker leather used to make combat boots. Boots can be polished with a waxy paste polish for a high gloss, but men's dress shoes should be treated to a high-quality cream polish.

Remove the laces, then wipe the shoe with a clean cotton cloth to remove any surface dirt or dust. Apply a thin coat of polish and let it dry. Use a brush to remove the bulk of the polish (be sure to get any polish out of the lace holes and indentations in wing tips), then buff with a soft cloth. Use liquid edge dressing to blacken the sides of the soles, right below the uppers, if needed.

---

*Activity:* Practice polishing shoes. If possible, watch a professional shoe shiner work.

---

Cowboy boots should be treated like fine shoes, unless they are made of an unusual material, like snake or alligator, in which case you should check with the manufacturer about cleaning procedures. Be sure to match polish colors carefully.

Many work, engineer, and motorcycle boots have a oily surface that isn't really meant to take a shine. In fact, if you use saddle soap, you can remove this water-resistant coating and render the boot useless in damp conditions. Instead, use a brush to remove any caked-on dirt, and wipe the boot with a damp cloth as needed. Some boots can be treated with a leather conditioner like Lexol. Again, it is best to check with the individual manufacturer.

Leather accessories like wallets and belts can be cleaned with a very small amount of cream polish in a matching color.

> *Suggested Reading: Leather and Latex Care: How to Keep Your Leather and Latex Looking Great* by Kelly J. Thibault is a great guide to caring for dress and fetish leathers.

> *Resources:* Many local BDSM organizations and national leather conferences sponsor occasional workshops on bootblacking.

**The gentleman's gentleman: public services for the private man**

If you're familiar with Jeeves, the cool, collected, and very correct manservant to Bertie Wooster in P. G. Wodehouse's frothy comic novels, then you will know that a valet will often have more on his hands than shoe polish. Jeeves – definitely the brains in the Wooster operation – routinely handles both mundane affairs, like luncheons and shopping, for his hapless master, while effortlessly averting social disasters.

While most valets don't face the challenges that Jeeves does – most masters being better endowed in gray matter than old Bertie W – you should be prepared to deal with minor matters of household organizing and basic secretarial duties.

*Activity:* Read one of Wodehouse's Jeeves novels: *Life With Jeeves,* published by Penguin, is an omnibus edition including *Right Ho Jeeves, The Inimitable Jeeves,* and *Very Good Jeeves.* Make a list of all the tasks that Jeeves is charged with in the space of one novel. (You needn't include all the comedy-of-errors plots, just the domestic and secretarial tasks.) Then read the appropriate lessons in this book if you don't yet feel equal to the tasks described.

*Suggested Reading:* For a well-rounded sense of the tradition of the manservant, the Lord Peter Wimsey mysteries of Dorothy Sayers are as indispensable as Wodehouse's novels. See also the titles suggested in the lesson on Butlers.

# Lesson 36. The personal secretary

Before "longtime companions" and "significant others," the term "personal secretary" was a euphemism for "lover." Although officially society did not condone non-marital relationships, polite company acknowledged the (often young and attractive) men and women who shared their famous lovers' lives with this sobriquet. Often the person in question was more of an escort than a secretary, but sometimes they did indeed attend to their partner's papers and business calls.

Why would someone with considerable business skills choose the life of a slave over the life of a capitalist? For the same reason that other educated, upwardly mobile people might choose to spend their time dressed as French maids or butlers: they enjoy being of service to another person.

In fact, the role of personal secretary is ideal for people who need to earn an income, but prefer to work at home, or whose dominant companion runs a business and needs help. (Think of the many "mom and pop" businesses, run by husband-and-wife teams, for example.) Personal secretaries may want to keep their professional skills up to par, or may simply prefer working in a professional setting rather than in household service. Dominants who work as writers or artists often appreciate help with the business side of their careers, so they have more freedom to create. In any case, this sometimes overlooked submissive role, when executed with care, provides a wonderful alternative to the more traditional maid- or man-servant or sex slave roles.

The bywords of personal assistants are Efficiency and Discretion. Since the dominant's livelihood may in part depend on your performance, you will be expected to act in a professional manner when on the job. While in the office (or on the phone) you are Mr. Jones' assistant, at least as far as his clients or customers are concerned. You must take care not to allow any emotions to interfere with your job performance. (See "Business Ethics and Slavehood" for more on this topic.)

Highly organized and able slaves – who are well-suited to the personal secretary role – may have a difficult time maintaining an appropriate sense of submission while working. There is no contradiction between being competent and being of service, as the many businesspersons who would be utterly lost without their secretaries will tell you. Just as a housekeeper must be respectful and friendly with suppliers but submissive to his or her Owner, a personal secretary can project an air of confident professionalism to clients, while showing deference to the Owner.

---

*Exercise:* Write or rework your résumé as if you were applying to be a dominant's personal secretary. What special categories of information might you include? What skills would you emphasize? What skills might you hope to gain?

---

*Suggested Reading: The Professional Secretary's Handbook (3rd ed.)* and *The Professional Secretary's Management Skills* by John Spencer and Adrian Pruss are excellent guides to business etiquette and protocoL

### Telephone etiquette

Miss Abernathy notes with dismay the decline of proper telephone etiquette, both in the public and private arenas. As a personal secretary, you will often need to make business (and perhaps personal) calls for the dominant. Please remember that your tone and style of presentation on the telephone reflect on the dominant.

---

*Activity:* When you make calls for yourself, practice these steps. (If you are calling a shop for information only, you can even pretend to be calling on behalf of someone else.)

1) Always identify yourself with your full name. (Unfortunately, these days you can no longer expect the person on the other end of the line to return the favor, although in most circumstances, they should.)

2) Mention that you are calling on behalf of Mr/Ms. X (the dominant) if this information is relevant. (It will be, for example, if you are making reservations at a restaurant.)

3) State the purpose of your call as simply and directly as possible: This is John Smith. I'm calling on behalf of Mr. Brown, who is a patient of Dr. Lowry's. Mr. Brown would like to make an appointment with the doctor for next Thursday.

4) When leaving a message on an answering machine or voicemail, spell your name and repeat your phone number (and area code, if necessary) twice. Speak slowly and clearly, over-pronouncing numbers.

5) Avoid casual language: "yeah" and "hey" have no place in a business call, particularly if you are not personally acquainted with the speaker. Never say "hunh?" or "what?' if you haven't heard something clearly. The latter can sound too curt and the former, Neanderthal. Say "Would you repeat that please?" or 'What did you say, please?" instead. Never use profanity, even if you are angry or the other party has used it first. (If faced with an angry caller, it is professional to react with even more formality, not less.)

6) If you have received help from someone who has not identified him- or herself by name, it is appropriate to ask, "With whom am I speaking, please?' Then thank the person for their help, using their name: "Thank you, Lisa, I appreciate your help today."

## Writing letters

After telephoning, the most common task for personal secretaries is letter-writing. The personal letter is a dying art, and the business letter is often mired in mumbo-jumbo and cliché.

Be as clear and direct as possible, while avoiding unnecessary information that may confuse the reader. Check the letter carefully for grammar and spelling errors, and refer to a standard secretarial manual if you are in doubt about forms of address or style.

---

*Exercise:* Write a business-style letter requesting information on a product or service you have seen advertised in the newspaper.

---

*Exercise:* Write a formal thank-you note for a gift you have recently received. (Consider writing a thank-you note to your trainer!)

---

Newer technologies, like email, have changed business writing styles dramatically. Some things remain consistent, however. An electronic medium does not give the user the right to ignore common courtesy; in fact, it requires knowledge of a special set of social graces sometimes referred to as "netiquette." Particularly when corresponding by email for business, observe the standard form of the business letter as closely as possible: use standard spelling, capitalization, and punctuation; end with your full name, title, and company name; and provide an email address to which the recipient of your mail can respond. Finally, you should be aware that commercial messages are unwelcome on most newsgroups, mailing lists, and bulletin boards.

**Suggested Reading: If your handwriting could stand some improvement, you may benefit from *Write Now* by Getty and Dubay and *Teach Yourself Better Handwriting* by Sassoon and Briem. *How to Write First-Class Letters* by L. Sue Baugh, *The Art of Letter Writing* by Lassor A. Blumenthal, and *Lifetime Encyclopedia of Letters* by Harold F. Meyer, revised and expanded edition, are all helpful guides to correspondence.**

## Office organization

In some ways, managing an office is not unlike managing a house. Your success depends on your ability to plan ahead, minimize waste, and maximize productivity while maintaining a comfortable, pleasant environment for all.

If you have enough storage space, try to buy office supplies in bulk; you'll almost always save money.

---

*Activity:* Review the process for creating a Master Grocery List in the Household Management section of this book. Now create an Master Supply List for your office. (See the *Suggested Reading* for some hints.) Then, following the instructions in the lesson for Housekeepers, create a Price Book for office supplies. Compare prices both at a small local stationery store and at an office supply superstore.

---

**Suggested Reading: *Organizing Your Home Office for Success* by Lisa Kanarek is the single best title on this topic. It covers everything from home office designs to filing systems.**

## Time management

To keep your work on track, you'll need to use "To Do" lists. A simple wall calendar with sufficient space to write (for long-range planning) and a loose-leaf binder filled with 8 1/2 x 11 paper are all you really need.

---

*Activity:* On your wall calendar, enter due dates and appointments: June 12: Bailiwick project due; June 13: Mr. Jones haircut, 3 p.m. You can also use a large appointment book, but be sure that it allows you to see at least one month at a time.

---

*Activity:* For your daily "To Do" list, follow these steps.

1) Label a blank sheet of paper with the date.

2) Check the calendar to see if there are any deadlines or appointments. Write them at the top of the page.

3) Next, check to see what projects may be due in 1, 2, 3, and 4 weeks. These will, in all likelihood, form the basis of your tasks for the day, with projects due in one week commanding more attention than projects due later.

4) Now write down the specific tasks you want to get done: type Bailiwick letter, phone accountant, reconfirm flight reservations... Try to group similar activities together: make all your phone calls at one time, when possible.

5) Prioritize your tasks by numbering them from most pressing to least pressing. (You will also want to identify which tasks may not need attention at all: Some problems simply resolve themselves with time.)

6) Begin with the most pressing task and work steadily through your list.

You may prefer to use a commercial personal planning system. These can be very helpful, but keep in mind that they should make your work easier, not more difficult. If you find you spend more time fussing with your planner than working, find a simpler system. The *Suggested Reading* will help you create one that works for you. Of course, you will also need to consider the dominant's work style and planning needs, too. Find out if s/he prefers a specific system and try to work with that.

## Business ethics and slavehood

Undoubtedly you've heard the old adage that forbids mixing business and pleasure. But a slave who works in his or her Owner s business is doing just that. How can you maintain a solid working relationship while acknowledging your respective roles in each other's lives?

The answer should by now be familiar: communicate. When you are making your preliminary arrangement for a slave contract, spell out the boundaries between work and play, between public and private, in detail. Whatever makes you feel efficient and competent, you should have in this case. It may be a simple change in modes of address: you call her "Mistress" in the house, but "Ms. Jones" in the office, and she calls you "slave" after hours, but "Miss Smith" at work. The titles signal a temporary change of role in response to the new, more public setting.

If you have been trained not to speak unless spoken to, you may have to arrange a sign, if only for yourself, that allows you to speak more freely in the office. Perhaps you can arrange a ritual with the Owner in which he places his hand over your mouth and then removes it, saying, "Speak at will, until I tell you otherwise." Even something so simple, an acknowledgment of your special relationship, can help you make the transition from slave to secretary.

With more and more home-based businesses and telecommuters, the lines between business and pleasure are being blurred. With some communication, you can avoid the pitfalls of the office romance while maintaining your sense of submission.

---

*Exercise:* Devise a ritual that you think would help you make the transition from private to public more smoothly. If appropriate, share this ritual with your trainer, or keep a copy in your slave journal.

---

*Further Training:* See the lessons on Escorts and Butlers.

*Suggested Reading:* Although it is addressed primarily to aspiring executives in traditional work environments, *Molloy's Live for Success* contains some useful observations on the unspoken rules of corporate culture. It will be helpful if you are doing business in a conservative field.

*Resources:* Your local business college, vocational training centet or community college no doubt offers a wide range of courses to improve your clerical and general secretarial skills.

# Advanced Studies

Congratulations on completing the Area Studies section of the course. By now you will have attained a deeper knowledge of your own skills and talents and will have chosen one or more areas of specialization.

At this point, you may be considering a greater commitment to this life. Many slaves fantasize about a full-time, "live-in" relationship that will allow them to live as a slave without interruption. It is possible to arrange a "24/7" (i.e., 24 hours a day, 7 days a week) contract, but it should not be entered into lightly.

The lessons that follow will help you examine some of the issues that arise as you contemplate this step. We will also cover some related subjects, such as permanent marks, serving multiple owners, and training other slaves. Finally, in preparation for your final project, we will explore in more detail how a slave can live ethically in submission to another person.

Again, congratulations on your work to this point, and best of luck as you approach the end of the course.

# Lesson 44. Live-in arrangements I: pragmatic considerations

If you are considering a live-in arrangement, there are any number of issues you must review before signing or even negotiating a contract with a dominant.

---

*Exercise:* Choose the answer that best reflects your ideas.

1.  As a live-in, I'd live at...
    a.  our house.
    b.  his/her house.
    c.  an in-law apartment at his/her house.
2.  I'd earn my living...
    a.  at the same lob I had before.
    b.  Those days are over. Master provides for me now.
    c.  doing part-time work for Master's business.
3.  We'll have...
    a.  a joint checking account.
    b.  a custodial account in Mistress's name.
    c.  my own checking and savings accounts.
4.  After signing a contract, I could move in with Master...
    a.  Move in? I already live here!
    b.  any time. As long as he pays the movers, of course.
    c.  once I settled my affairs and put my things in storage.
5.  The best thing about a live-in contract is...
    a.  formalizing our D/S relationship.
    b.  giving up complete control of my affairs.
    c.  being able to work at home and still be a slave.
6.  Mistress is...

a. employed outside the home, as am I.

b. easily able to provide for both of us.

c. self-employed.

7. My only dependents are...

a. my grown children.

b. my goldfish.

c. my dog.

8. What I enjoy most about submission is...

a. how well Master and I complement each other.

b. feeling completely in Master's hands.

c. being useful and competent.

9. When I file my taxes, I use...

a. the 1040A form.

b. the 1040EZ form.

c. the 1040 form with the SE and C schedules.

10. The car is registered...

a. in both our names.

b. in Mistress's name.

c. in my name.

11. The answering machine says...

a. "the Jones residence"

b. "Mr. Jones' residence"

c. "Press one for Mr. Jones. Press two for Miss Smith..."

12. If I weren't a slave, I'd be...

a. gainfully employed. Gotta pay the rent!

b. socking away my income.... know a good broker?

c. building up my own business.

13. The neighbors think...

a. ' we're swinger types.

b. I'm a gold digger.

    c.   I'm his secretary.

14.    Our arrangement makes me feel...

    a.   loved.

    b.   desired.

    c.   needed.

15.    The hardest part of our arrangement is...

    a.   keeping our roles going day-to-day.

    b.   worrying about how I'd manage if Mistress threw me out.

    c.   remembering my place.

---

If you chose mostly (a) answers, you would do well with the partnership model. You are probably already in a committed relationship with a dominant, or are in the process of exploring dominance and submission with your long-term partner. While you're serious about submission, you recognize that financial necessity and the other commitments you may have to family prevent you from giving up your job. You prefer that your D/S relationship be private (perhaps you share your status with some close friends who may also be "in the scene"). You don't care if you retain some control over your day-to-day affairs, since your role as a slave is more about how you feel about your partner and how the two of you work together. You may want to experiment with other styles of submission. For example, the two of you can rent a hotel room or cabin for a Master/Mistress and slave weekend.

If you chose mostly (b) answers, you are most attracted to the dependent model. While this model is the one most often depicted in BDSM fiction, it is relatively rare in real life. Most households require two incomes to function, but if either you or the dominant has sufficient assets, this model may work for you. There are two major caveats: first, slavehood is not a substitute for employment. If you have trouble holding down a job, you will find it difficult to be a slave, as slavehood involves even more personal responsibility than most paid jobs. Second, get it in writing. If you are turning over assets to a dominant, Miss Abernathy strongly recommends that you contact a lawyer to draw up a pre-nuptial (or domestic partnership) agreement that spells out in detail what you are bringing to the household and what is due you should it dissolve. Both parties should have current wills as well. You may also want to agree upon a way of safeguarding your prospects should you need to return to outside employment. The dominant may be willing to refer to you as a "personal assistant" for job search purposes.

If you chose mostly (c) answers, you are best suited for the employee model. You come to the relationship with considerable business skills, and you want to retain some amount of autonomy and control over your work. The dominant may work from home and engage you part-time as an assistant or consultant. This model can be challenging to your submission, as it is sometimes hard to switch from super-efficient businessperson to "lowly" slave after hours. Also, by linking your work life to your personal life, you run the risk of losing both if one goes sour. Still, if you enjoy feeling needed and are secure in your abilities, this model may be workable for you.

# Lesson 45. Live-in arrangements II: financial considerations

The diagnostic test in the last lesson should have given you some idea of the financial realities that live-in slaves face. Depending on the type of arrangement you enter into – partnership, dependent, or employee – you may have to make some important changes in your financial situation.

*Activity:* (Note: Consider hiring a financial professional to help you with this exercise.) Take stock of your financial situation. What is your net worth? Are you in debt? Are you in default on any loans or consumer debts (credit cards)? If you were to quit work today, how long would you be able to cover your (current) expenses? What is the minimum amount of money you think you could live on? Do you expect to inherit any money? Do you own valuables like jewelry, antiques, art...?

*Suggested Reading: Get a Financial Life* by Beth Kobliner is a straightforward introduction to personal finance. Though written with younger people in mind, it will be useful to all.

*Activity:* Make a list of all your accounts, investments, and valuable property. Have this document notarized and put it in a safe deposit box.

*Activity:* Design a budget based on your desired live-in status. Don't forget necessities like health insurance as well as any uniforms, toiletries, and other needs. How could you simplify your lifestyle and cut down expenses?

*Suggested Reading:* Elaine St. James has authored several little volumes on simple living which provide hundreds of money-saving tips.

Talking about money isn't very romantic, but it is one of the most often overlooked aspects of slave training and in relationships of all kinds. If money becomes a source of conflict in your negotiations, please take the time to discuss not just the dollars-and-cents particulars, but your feelings about money itself. How was money handled in your family of origin? How important is it to you to have money in your pocket? Do you feel uncomfortable if you don't have next month's rent in the bank by the 15th? What does money symbolize to you: security? freedom? status? By talking frankly about your feelings, you will be better able to negotiate a mutually agreeable way to handle finances in your relationship.

# Lesson 46. Live-in arrangements III: emotional considerations

In the last two lessons, we have already begun to look at some of the emotional ramifications of live-in arrangements. Before proceeding with this lesson, please review the following lessons: "Assessing Strengths and Weaknesses," "Assessing Risk," and "What Kind of Slave Am I?" You may want to do the exercises in these lessons again, now that you have a broader knowledge of the responsibilities of a slave.

While the exercises here are brief, they are meant to be completed slowly. Take your time, and write as much as you need to. Then share your responses with your trainer or dominant, as appropriate.

---

*Exercise:* Name the emotions that you feel when you think about the prospect of a live-in arrangement.

---

*Exercise:* In your slave journal, write a list of your fears regarding a live-in relationship. Do not censor yourself. All your "silly" fears are legitimate and valid. Be prepared to share these fears with your prospective Owner in a candid fashion and to think of ways to allay them.

---

*Exercise:* Using the 1.10 exercise in "Assessing Risk," write at least a paragraph on the subject "Being 'Out' as a Slave." How does other people's awareness of your status affect you, your Owner, and others in your life?

Does a live-in arrangement change that awareness? How do you feel about the possibility of criticism from family, friends, or authority figures? If you are uncomfortable with being "out," what measures would you need to take to safeguard your privacy? What limits might this place on your relationships?

# Lesson 47. Permanent marks: piercing

In the Manual I discussed a variety of ways that dominants may choose to physically mark their slaves as a sign of ownership, commitment, and devotion. Here we will focus on the method most commonly associated with slavehood: piercing.

*Exercise:* Complete the following sentences:
The kind of piercing I like the most is...
I'm afraid of being pierced because...
People who have piercings...
If s/he saw my piercing, my physician would...
It s/he saw my piercing, my best friend would...
If they knew I was pierced, my family members would...
If I were pierced, I would be embarrassed to...
Erotically, piercing would...
Piercing would affect my submission by...

Note: If you are considering another form of permanent marking, like a tattoo, branding, or scarification (cutting), use this exercise by substituting the name of your preferred method of marking.

*Exercise:* In your slave journal, write about the associations that permanent body piercings have to you.

Do you have any body piercings? Why did you choose them? Did they mark a particular event in your life? How do you feel about them now? Have you ever let a piercing heal over? Why? If you have no piercings, do you know anyone who does? Have you seen pictures of piercings? How did they make you feel?

*Activity:* Visit a professional piercer. (Most major North American cities have at least one.) Many will have printed information for you to take home, and they'll be happy to talk with you about their techniques and training. (Reputable body piercers will not use piercing guns, will have an autoclave, and will not recommend sterling silver jewelry for body piercings.) If there is no piercer in your area, or if you feel uncomfortable with your local piercer, it is much better to wait until you can visit San Francisco, New York, Los Angeles, Amsterdam, London, or Paris, all of which have many well-trained, responsible piercers.

*Suggested Reading: Story of O* by Pauline Reage. How does O interpret her rings? What do they mean to her?

*Resources:* Fakir Musafar periodically teaches workshops for intermediate to advanced piercers; information is available at www.fakir.org/classes/index.html.

# Lesson 48. Serving multiple owners

While most of this book has been written with the assumption that you will be serving one other individual, it is now time to look at another possibility: serving multiple owners. Most often, this involves serving a couple, but it may also include a ménage of three or more.

If you are considering the possibility of serving a couple or a ménage, you face some special challenges. First, you may be worked harder, since tasks tend to increase exponentially with the number of people you serve. Second, you may find yourself struggling with favoritism (your own and the Owners'). Third, you may be caught in a conflict of wills, as when one Owner wants a task performed a certain way and the other wants it done differently or not at all. Finally, your status as slave may be dependent on the stability of your Owners' relationship. If their arrangement ends, how will it affect you?

Serving multiple owners does have some distinct advantages as well. You may get more individual attention and care, including more sex, if that is part of your arrangement. You will have a chance to develop more flexibility and better communication skills. You may experience a greater variety of types of service, as the different owners express different needs. You will benefit by the different training styles and experiences that the owners may exhibit. You will also have the privilege of witnessing an intimate relationship as the partners weather the seasons and changes that life brings.

---

*Exercise:* Write a short essay on the theme of "Polyfidelity." (Some people prefer this term to "non-monogamy" as a way to refer to multiple committed relationships. For more information, see the *Suggested Reading* list.) What does the word suggest to you? What qualities would you need to bring to such a relationship? What challenges would it present to you personally?

---

*Exercise:* List five special things that you might need to negotiate for in a contract between you and a couple.

*Activity:* If possible, talk with someone involved in a long-term polyamorous relationship. (If you don't know anyone in this situation, please explore the *Suggested Reading* carefully and, if you have Internet access, read the newsgroup alt.polyamory for a while.) What difficulties have they encountered? How do they deal with conflict? What advantages do they see in their relationship? What advice do they have for you?

*Suggested Reading: The Ethical Slut* by Dossie Easton and Catherine A. Liszt is a sensible, BDSM-friendly guide to multiple relationships of all sorts. Other titles dealing with polyamory (multiple love relationships) and polyfidelity are *Loving More: The Polyfidelity Primer,* by Ryam Nearing, *Redefining Our Relationships: Guidelines for Responsible Open Relationships,* by Wendy O Matik, and *Polyamory: The New Love Without Limits* by Deborah Anapol.

# Lesson 49. Training others

One of the greatest displays of confidence that a dominant can make is to allow an experienced slave to train a new submissive. The dominant may not have time to attend to new slaves-in-training or may feel that an experienced servant can better prepare them for their roles. Sometimes, in the course of training, it becomes apparent that a slave, while happily and willingly submissive to the Owner, may also have a dominant side that requires expression. Further, some service roles described above, like housekeepers and butlers, are essentially household managers, and as such require the ability to train underlings. In all of these cases, the opportunity to train another person may fill a slave with pride and expectant joy.

If you are asked to train a slave yourself, you must take time and care to determine if you are equal to the task. You should also carefully examine your feelings: are you likely to feel jealous of the newcomer? If you are experiencing any frustrations in your own submission, you may find yourself taking them out on your trainee, or subtly undermining your own training efforts. It may help you to know that many experienced dominants were once, themselves, slaves. If this is the case with your Owner, you may be able to speak frankly with him or her and derive some measure of reassurance from his or her experiences.

---

*Exercise:* Write down any fears that you have about training a new slave. No fear is "too silly"; all are valid. You may want to use your meditation time to explore some of these fears.

---

*Activity:* Read back over your slave journal from start to finish. What obstacles, internal or external, did you face when you began your training? How did you overcome them? Which do you still consider troubling?

---

Remember that if you have worked your way steadily though this study course, you now have a great wealth of experience to draw on. You know yourself better than many people do, and you are better able to articulate your ideas and feelings. Perhaps you have even felt the stirrings of a spiritual dimension to your submission. These are gifts; share them freely.

**Suggested Reading: Review the basic BDSM texts listed in the introduction to the Sex Slave section.**

# Lesson 50. Ethical slavehood

When asked to explain their desires, many submissives will say that they enjoy letting go of responsibility for their actions, if only for a time. It is true that the burdens of life can weigh heavily on our shoulders, and it is refreshing to feel the lightness and freedom of childhood when we needed only do as we were told for the world to seem a bright and safe place.

However, by now I hope you have come to see slavehood as more than escapism. As a slave, you do not give up your will. You learn to attune it to another person's, until the two are as one. This is the real source of that "second sense" that some experienced slaves have: they know their Owners so well that they experience the Owners' needs and desires as their own. In a sense, then, rather than giving up responsibility, a slave becomes doubly accountable.

Undoubtedly you will encounter minor circumstances in which you are called upon to act against your better judgment. After all, intimate relationships often require us to set aside our own desires in favor of our partner's preferences, at least once in a while. Sometimes these requests are illogical, but their importance rests in the realm of emotions, and so we act. This is all the more true in dominant/submissive relationships.

And yet we are still people, frail in our humanity. Dominants are not all-powerful; slaves are not omniscient. Further, even in the most well-planned lives, reality rudely intrudes. How do you, as a slave, maintain a firm ethical foundation when your will and that of the Owner are at odds?

In the following exercise, I ask you to spend some time thinking carefully about how you would respond to some difficult situations. Write about your thoughts and doubts in your slave journal. There are no right answers here; each of these situations involves moral ambiguity, with plenty of shades of gray. Please share your ahswers with your trainer and be prepared to discuss them frankly.

---

*Exercise:* How would you respond to these situations? What might you do to prevent them? Can you imagine circumstances that might make other choices understandable and acceptable, for yourself or others?

1. Your contract stipulates safer sex. One night, your Owner orders you to "forget the condom." What do you do?

2. Your Owner asks you to purchase illegal drugs for his/her use. What do you do?

3. You are a personal secretary, and you become aware that your Owner is committing tax fraud. What do you do?

4. Your Owner is a non-custodial parent. Just a few minutes before the child is due to arrive for a weekend visit, the Owner orders you to strip for sex. What do you do?

5. Your contract allows for you to be lent out to your Owner's dominant friends. Recently your Owner has become close with someone about whom you've heard negative gossip that leads you to believe they may be dangerous. Now your Owner wants to lend you to this person. What do you do?

6. Some close friends of your Owner's visit. After their departure, you discover that some money is missing. What do you do?

7. Your contract stipulates that you and your Owner will have unprotected sex only with each other. You have kept your word, but

you discover you have contracted an STD. What do you do?

8. One of the Owner's credit cards is missing. You know you didn't touch it, but the Owner accuses you. What do you do?

9. You become aware that your Owner is developing a bad reputation in your local BDSM community. What do you do?

10. Your Owner beats you non-consensually. You leave the relationship. Soon after, you hear that a novice submissive is seeing your former Owner. What do you do?

Submission has sometimes been referred to as "consensual co-dependency." From the outside, a dominant/submissive relationship may appear emotionally unbalanced, even abusive. With consent as an ethical bottom line, however, BDSM practitioners are able to enjoy power play without undermining any participant's essential human rights. Even as a slave, you do retain those rights, morally and legally.

**Suggested Reading: *How to Be an Adult: A Handbook on Psychological and Spiritual Interaction* by David Richo outlines a program for building good boundaries, dealing with difficult emotions, and promoting self-esteem. This is an excellent guide, even for therapy "veterans."**

# Final Project

My heartfelt congratulations to you! You have completed your training course and are ready to put together your final project. The final project is a major undertaking, in your special field of interest, that displays your knowledge and achievement in that field.

If you are working with a trainer, he or she will make suggestions for a final project. If you are working alone, you may choose an appropriate project for yourself.

Take your time in choosing and completing the project. (I suggest two to three weeks.) If possible, the project should be at least semi-public, but you may "serve" a willing friend if no dominant is available to you.

Some suggestions for final projects:

- Butlers can arrange a small dinner party for a friend.
- Ladies' maids can give a friend a makeover.
- Escorts can accompany a friend to the opera.
- Housekeepers can spring-clean a friend's house.
- Personal secretaries can offer to organize a self-employed friend's home office.
- Sex slaves can offer a massage (erotic or not) to a friend.

Do not feel limited by these suggestions. By giving of yourself, even in a friendly way, you are honoring your submissive nature and creating good will. What greater gift do we have to offer?

# Conclusion

As we end our time together, please take some time to review all that you have accomplished since you began this course. I hope that you have come to feel, as I do, that slavehood is a noble and honorable path.

You may find yourself excited about the path ahead of you. If you are still searching for a dominant to serve, take heart in the fact that your dedication to bettering yourself through self-directed training can only make you more attractive to those who know the value of service. If you are already in service, I wish you all the delights and wonders that this path may bring. A slave's training is never really finished, as there is always some new skill, some new specialty that draws you onward.

Until we meet again, I remain, etc.

*Christina Abernathy (Miss)*

# Appendix A: A D/S reading list

Nothing has done more to propagate and perpetuate the dream of erotic slavehood than literature. Miss Abernathy has no objections to erotica; in fact, I encourage my submissives to read everything they can get their hands on. I'd like to take a brief look at some of the literary sources of D/S fantasies and realities.

**The Marquis de Sade.** Sade was a remarkable figure and well worth reading if only to explore the expressions of an obsessive, encyclopedic brain. *The Hundred and One Days of Sodom* is a literal catalog of pain and pleasure, and *Justine* and its companion novel, *Juliette,* provide the basis for much modern BDSM literature. Yet, most twentieth-century readers will be disappointed by Sade's work. Sade fancied himself a philosopher, and, when it would get him out of the Bastille, a revolutionary. Sade's slaves are invariably young, beautiful noble-things with exotic faux antique names; the masters are often old and repulsive clergymen and whores. But if you enjoy graphic depictions of coprophilia, copious buggery and religious blasphemy, you'll love Sade.

**Leopold von Sacher-Masoch: *Venus In Furs.*** More to the point is the work of Leopold von Sacher-Masoch, a nineteenth-century Austrian novelist. The author of *Venus In Furs,* Sacher-Masoch was notorious in his own time as a decadent and deviant soul. It is to him that we owe the D/S contract, the use of "slave names," the integration of fetish and D/S, the archetypal female-dominant/male-submissive relationship, and the term "masochism." In psychiatric literature, "masochism" refers to behavior and desires that we would call "submissive" today; modern BDSM players often use "masochist" specifically to refer to a person who finds erotic satisfaction in physical sensation ("pain").

**Pauline Réage: *Story of O*.** In 1954, a novel appeared that was to change the face of erotic literature forever. It told the story of the erotic enslavement of a French fashion photographer known only as O. Taken by her lover, René, to a chateau on the outskirts of Paris, O is introduced to an exclusive society of dominant men and women and their female sex slaves. Slowly she becomes involved in the Chateau's society and comes to recognize herself as a slave.

O has come to typify the role of the sex slave: willing and available, suggestible and passionate. It also introduced the theme of erotic marking. At different points in the book, O receives labia piercings and a brand that mark her as a slave. In short, *Story of O* set the standard for male-dominant/female-submissive erotica.

**Anne Rice: *Exit to Eden* and the *Sleeping Beauty* trilogy.** This prolific author may be most famous for her vampire books, but she also wrote a number of pseudonymous erotic novels with strong BDSM themes. *Exit To Eden* is set on an island resort for the rich and submissive. Dominant trainer Lisa finds her match in client Elliot. This rather serious novel was made into a comic film. Even more notorious than *Exit to Eden* is the *Sleeping Beauty* trilogy *(The Claiming of Sleeping Beauty, Beauty's Punishment,* and *Beauty's Release)*. These erotic fairy tales recount the enslavement of the princess Beauty and her subsequent adventures at the hands of a bevy of dominant noblefolk. They feature many scenes of erotic domination, including human ponies and sexual torture devices.

**John Preston:** *Mr. Benson.* What *Story of O* did for the male-dominant/female-submissive erotic imagination, John Preston's *Mr. Benson* did for gay men. This story of a young man's initiation into the world of D/S originally appeared in serial form in *Drummer* magazine and made Preston the object of adulation. "I enjoyed writing *Mr. Benson*," Preston explained in his essay, "Flesh and the Word: My Life with Pornography," "but I didn't write it with a serious intent, no matter how seriously people took it eventually."

In many ways, *Mr. Benson* parallels *Story of O.* The dominant is extraordinarily wealthy and very mysterious. What begins as mere sexual attraction, ends, for the submissive, in a complete change of lifestyle. Despite its sensationalistic climax – white slavery, indeed! – *Mr. Benson* is an undisputed classic of gay male BDSM erotica.

**Pat Califia:** *Macho Sluts, Doc and Fluff, Melting Point.* If John Preston brought gay D/S out of the closet, Pat (now Patrick) Califia did the same for lesbians. A longtime leather community activist and educator, Califia has penned two short story collections, *Macho Sluts* and *Melting Point*; a novel, *Doc and Fluff*; an introduction to S/M play for couples, *Sensuous Magic*; a guide to lesbian sexuality, *Sapphistry*; and a collection of essays on sexual politics, *Public Sex.* He has also edited such groundbreaking anthologies as *Coming To Power* and *Doing It For Daddy.* Many of these stories explore sexual taboos – incest, vampiristic bloodlust, cross-orientation sex, rape, and addiction – with honesty and artistry. Califia's work is essential reading for anyone interested in BDSM.

**Laura Antoniou: the *Marketplace* series.** Among the recent additions to the literature of D/S is the Marketplace series by

Laura Antoniou. Originally written under the pseudonym "Sara Adamson," Antoniou's fiction – *The Marketplace, The Slave, The Trainer, The Acaemy* and *The Reunion* – represents some of the finest BDSM erotica today. Antoniou imagines a "slave society," not wholly unlike Reage's Chateau or Rice's exotic-erotic island resort, but exposes the inner workings of that society. In addition to the Marketplace books, Antoniou has edited a number of anthologies, including *Leatherwomen, Leatherwomen II, By Her Subdued,* and *Some Women.*

**Other Titles.** There are many other special interest BDSM titles available. Unfortunately, many of them are poorly written; some are bowdlerized classics. Here are some further suggestions for your library.

*The Pearl* is a collection of Victorian erotic stories and poems, many of them containing scenes of "domestic discipline."

*Harriet Marwood, Governess (Anon.)* is classic Victoriana for those with a taste for the birch.

*Miss High Heels* will appeal to sissy maids and other cross-dressers.

The *Gor* novels, a science fiction series that runs to many volumes, is set in a male-dominated society. If you can ignore the passages that tout male social supremacy, the novels can be quite enjoyable.

Artemis Oakgrove has written the *Throne Trilogy,* urban fantasies featuring a wealthy butch lesbian and her slaves.

David Aaron Clark, author of The Marquis de Sade's *Juliette: Vengeance on the Lord,* has shown himself to be a promising writer of BDSM novels.

# Appendix B: Resource Guide

## General information

San Francisco Sex Information. www.sfsi.org, (415) 621-7300. Offers referrals and information on sex-related issues.

Kink-Aware Professionals. A free listing of kink-friendly psycho-therapeutic, medical, dental, alternative healing, or legal professionals, sponsored by the National Coalition for Sexual Freedom. www.ncsfreedom.org/kap/index.htm.

Society for Human Sexuality. An extensive website with articles, bibliographies and referrals on many forms of sexuality, both mainstream and alternative. www.sexuality.org.

## BDSM organizations

BDSM support groups, clubs and "munches" (informal meetings of kinky people in restaurants and, occasionally, bars) now exist in most American communities. Extensive national and international listings of BDSM organizations appear on many websites; one of the best is maintained by the Society of Janus at www.soj.org.

## BDSM events

BDSM events include conferences (anywhere from a couple of hundred attendees to thousands), sash competitions, single-day gatherings with speakers and a play party, weekend retreats both indoor and outdoor, and more. If you do not feel comfortable taking your slave or owner to a local venue, traveling together to a BDSM event can be a way to experience the heady feeling of being surrounded by fellow kinksters. A good calendar of upcoming events is maintained by the Society of Janus at www.soj.org.

# Appendix C: Selected Bibliography

Antoniou, Laura. The Marketplace. Mystic Rose Books, 2000.

–The Slave. Mystic Rose Books, 2001.

–The Trainer. Mystic Rose Books, 2001.

–The Academy: Tales of the Marketplace. Mystic Rose Books, 2000.

–The Reunion. Mystic Rose Books, 2003.

Albano, John R. Haircutting at Home. Berkley, 1995.

Allen, Christopher and Kimberly Burton Allen. A Butler's Life: Scenes from the Other Side of the Silver Salver. Beil, 1997.

Anand, Margo. The Art of Sexual Ecstasy. Tarcher/Putnam, 1989.

Anders, Charles. The Lazy Crossdresser. Greenery Press, 2002.

Anderson, Dan and Maggie Berman. Sex Tips for Straight Women from a Gay Man. HarperCollins, 1997.

Arnheim, Rudolph. Film as Art. U. of California Press, 1957.

Aslett, Don. The Cleaning Encyclopedia. Dell, 1993.

Aucoin, Kevyn. Making Faces. Little Brown, 1997.

Baldwin, Guy. SlaveCraft: Roadmaps for Erotic Servitude. Daedalus Publishing, 2002.

Bannon, Race. Learning the Ropes: A Basic Guide to Safe and Fun S/M Lovemaking. Daedalus Publishing, 1993.

Baugh, L Sue. How to Write First-Class Letters. NTC, 1994.

Bee, Jaymz and Jan Gregor. Cocktail Parties for Dummies. IDG, 1997.

Berkowitz, Bob. His Secret Life. Simon & Schuster, 1997.

Berthold-Bond. Clean & Green: The Complete Guide to Non-toxic and Environmentally Safe Housekeeping. Ceres, 1990.

–. The Green Kitchen Handbook. Harper Perennial, 1997.

Bespaloff, Alexis. Alexis Bespaloff's Complete Guide to Wine, rev. ed. Signet, 1994.

Blank, Joani, ed. I Am My Lover: Women Pleasure Themselves. Down There Press, 1997.

Blumenthal, Ussor A. The Art of Letter Writing. Perigee, 1977.

Bolton, Robert. People Skills. Touchstone, 1979.

Boostrom, Robert. Developing Creative & Critical Thinking: An Intergrated Approach. NTC, 1992.

Bornstein, Kate. My Gender Workbook. Routledge, 1998.

Boston Women's Health Book Collective. The New Our Bodies, Ourselves. Touchstone, 1992.

Boyden, Matthew. Opera: The Rough Guide. Rough Guides, 1997.

Boyles, Dennis et aL The Modern Man's Guide to Life. Harper Perennial, 1987.

Bride's Lifetime Guide to Good Food & Entertaining. Congdon & Weed, 1984.

Califia, Patrick. Sensuous Magic: A Guide to S/M for Adventurous Couples. 2nd ed. Cleis, 2003.

– ed. The Lesbian S/M Safety Manual. Lace, 1988.

– and Drew Campbell, eds. Bitch Goddess: the Spiritual Path of the Dominant Woman. Greenery, 1998.

Cameron, Julia and Mark Bryan. The Artist's Way: A Spiritual Path to Higher Creativity. Putnam, 1992.

Campbell, Jeff and the Clean Team. Speed Cleaning. Dell, 1997.

Casado, Matt A. Food and Beverage Service Guide. Wiley, 1994.

Cash, Thomas F. The Body Image Workbook. New Harbinger, 1997.

Child, Julia. The Way to Cook. Knopf, 1996.

Complete Book of Sewing. DK, 1996.

Corey, Kathy and Lynne Blackman. Rituals for the Bath. Warner, 1995.

Curtis, Lucy D. Lucy's List. Warner, 1995.

Davidson, Jeff. The Complete Idiot's Guide to Managing Your Time. Alpha Books, 1995.

Davis, Jonathan. Learn Bridge in a Weekend. Knopf, 1996.

Doner, Kalia and Margaret Doner. The Wellness Center's Spa at Home. Berkley, 1997.

Easton, Dossie and Catherine A. Liszt. The Ethical Slut: A Guide to Infinite Sexual Possibilities. Greenery, 1997.

– and Janet W. Hardy. The New Bottoming Book. Greenery Press, 2001.

– and Janet W. Hardy. The New Topping Book. Greenery Press, 2003.

– and Janet W. Hardy. Radical Ecstasy. Greenery Press, 2004.

Eisenberg, Ronni and Kate Kelly. The Overwhelmed Person's Guide to Time Management. Plume, 1997.

Flusser, Alan. Clothes and the Man: the Principles of Fine Men's Dress. Villard, 1994.

Fontanel, Beatrice. Support and Seduction: A History of Corsets and Bras. Abrams, 1997.

Fussell, Paul. Class: A Guide through the American Status System. Touchstone, 1983.

Gabor, Don. How to Start a Conversation and Make Friends. Fireside, 1983.

Gendler, J. Ruth. The Book of Qualities. Harper Perennial, 1988.

Gilford, Judith. The Packing Book: Secrets of the Carry-on Traveler. Ten Speed Press, 1996.

Gombrich, E.H. The Story of Art. 16th ed. Phaidon, 1995.

Greskovic, Robert. Ballet 101. Hyperion, 1998.

Gross, Kim Johnson et al. Woman's Face: Skin Care and Makeup. Knopf, 1997.

–. Work Clothes: Casual Dress for Serious Work. Knopf, 1996.

Henkin, Bill, and Sybil Holiday. Consensual Sadomasochism: How to Talk About It, And How to Do It Safely. Daedalus Publishing, 1996.

Hoffman, Miles. The NPR Classical Music Companion. Houghton Mifflin, 1997.

Human Kinetics with Thomas Hanlon, The Sports Rules Book. Human Kinetics, 1998.

Hynes, Angela. The Pleasures of Afternoon Tea. HP Books, 1987.

Ishiguro, Kazuo. The Remains of the Day. Vintage, 1993.

Jackson, Carole and Kalia Lulow. Color for Men. Ballantine, 1984.

Johnson, Carol A. Self-Esteem Comes in All Sizes. Main Street, 1995.

Jones, Judy and William Wilson. An Incomplete Education. Ballantine, 1995.

Kamman, Madeleine. The New Making of a Cook. Morrow, 1997.

Kanarek, Lisa. Organizing Your Home Office for Success. Plume, 1993.

Kent, Cassandra. Household Hints & Tips. DK, 1996.

– Organizing Hints & Tips. DK, 1997.

Klensch, Elsa. Style. Perigee, 1995.

Kobliner, Beth. Get a Financial Life. Fireside, 1996.

Lehmkuhl, Dorothy and Dolores Cotter Lamping. Organizing for the Creative Person. Crown, 1993.

MacMurray, Jessica M. and Allison Brewster Franzetti. The Book of 101 Opera Librettos. Black Dog & Leventhal, 1997.

Martin, Judith. Miss Manners' Guide to Excruciatingly Correct Behavior. Warner, 1982.

Meyer, Harold E. Lifetime Encyclopedia of Letters. rev. & exp. ed. Prentice Hall, 1992.

Miller, Phillip and Molly Devon. Screw the Roses, Send Me the Thorns. Mystic Rose, 1988.

Mitchell, Stewart. The Complete Illustrated Guide to Massage. Element, 1997.

Mitford, Nancy, ed. Noblesse Oblige: An Enquiry into the Identifiable Characteristics of the English Aristocracy. Atheneum, 1986.

Mittler, Gene and Rosalind Ragans. Understanding Art. Glencoe, 1992.

Molloy, John T. Molloy's Live for Success. Morrow, 1981.

Morehead, Albert H. et at. The New Complete Hoyle Revised. Doubleday, 1987.

Morin, Jack. Anal Pleasure and Health. Yes Press, 1986.

Mr. Boston Official Bartender's and Party Guide. 64th ed. Warner, 1994.

Murphy, Bruce, ed. Benét's Reader's Encyclopedia. HarperCollins, 1996.

Nagle, Jill, ed. Whores and Other Feminists. Routledge, 1997.

Nierenberg, Gerald I. and Henry H. Calero. How to Read a Person Like a Book. Pocket Books, 1971.

Ordesky, Maxine. The Complete Home Organizer. Grove, 1993.

Padwa, Lynette. Everything You Pretend to Know and Are Afraid Someone Will Ask. Penguin, 1996.

Piazza, Tom. The Guide to Classic Recorded Jazz. U of Iowa Press, 1995.

Plotkin, Fred. Opera 101. Hyperion, 1994.

Popov, Linda Kavelin. Sacred Moments: Daily Meditations on the Virtues. Plume, 1997.

Post, Elizabeth and Anthony Staffieri. The Complete Book of Entertaining. Harper & Row, 1981.

Post, Peggy. Emily Post's Etiquette. 16th ed. HarperCollins, 1997.

Preston, John. Mr. Benson. Cleis, 2004.

Professional Secretary's Handbook. 3rd ed. Houghton Mifflin, 1995.

Quant, Mary. Ultimate Makeup & Beauty. DK, 1996.

Queen, Carol. Exhibitionism for the Shy. Down There Press, 1995.

Réage, Pauline. Story of O. Ballantine, 1989.

Rinella, Jack. Becoming a Slave. Rinella Editorial Services, 2005.

– edited by Joseph W. Bean. The Compleat Slave. Daedalus Publishing, 1992.

– and Joseph W. Bean. The Master's Manual: A Handbook of Erotic Domianance. Daedalus Publishing, 1994.

– Partners In Power: Living In Kinky Relationships. Greenery Press, 2003.

Rombauer, Irma S. et al. Joy of Cooking. Scribner, 1997.

Rubenstein, Hal and Jim Mullen. Paisley Goes with Nothing: A Man's Guide to Style. Doubleday, 1995.

Sangster, Rob. Traveler's Tool Kit: How to Travel Absolutely Anywhere. Menasha Ridge Press, 1996.

Seirawan, Yasser. Play Winning Chess. Microsoft, 1995.

Seldon, Philip. The Complete Cigar Book. Ballantine, 1997.

–. The Pocket Idiot's Guide to Choosing Wine. Alpha, 1997.

Simon, Sidney B. In Search of Values. Warner, 1993. [0446394378]

Simpson, Helen. The London Ritz Book of Afternoon Tea. Arbor House, 1986.

Smith, Michael. The Afternoon Tea Book. Collier, 1986.

Spencer, John and Adrian Pruss. The Professional Secretary's Management Skills. Barron's, 1997.

Steiner, Claude and Paul Perry. Achieving Emotional Literacy. Avon, 1997.

Stewart, Martha. Entertaining. Clarkson Potter, 1982.

Strict, M.R. Intimate Invasion: The Erotic Ins & Outs of Enema Play. Greenery Press, 2004.

Sullivan, Lou. Information for the Female to Male Cross Dresser and Transsexual. 3rd ed. Ingersoll Gender Center, 1990.

Taormino, Tristan. The Ultimate Guide to Anal Sex for Women. Cleis, 1998.

Thibault, Kelly J. Leather and Latex Care: How to Keep Your Leather and Latex Looking Great. Daedalus, 1996.

Turner, E.S. What the Butler Saw. St. Martin's, 1962.

Veblen, Thorstein. The Theory of the Leisure Class. Penguin, 1994.

Vera, Veronica. Miss Vera's Finishing School for Boys Who Want to Be Girls. Main Street, 1997.

Warren, John. The Loving Dominant, 3rd edition. Greenery, 2007.

Waugh, Evelyn. Brideshead Revisited. Little Brown, 1945. [

Wertheimer, Neil, ed. Total Health for Men. Rodale Press, 1995.

Wiseman, Jay. Jay Wiseman's Erotic Bondage Handbook. Greenery Press, 2000.

– SM 101: A Realistic Introduction. 2nd ed. Greenery Press, 1996.

– Tricks: To Please a Man. Greenery Press, 2004.

– Tricks: To Please a Woman. Greenery Press, 2002.

Wodehouse, PG. Life with Jeeves. Penguin, 1981.

Wright, Jeni and Eric Treuillé. Le Cordon Bleu Complete Cooking Techniques. Morrow, 1996.

Yenawine, Philip. Key Art Terms for Beginners. Abrams, 1995.

Zilbergeld, Bernie. The New Male Sexuality. Bantam, 1992.

Zraly, Kevin. Windows on the World Complete Wine Course. Dell, 1985

## BDSM/KINK

**The Compleat Spanker**
Lady Green                                    $12.95

**Erotic Tickling**
Michael Moran                             $13.95

**Family Jewels**
Hardy Haberman                        $12.95

**Flogging**
Joseph W. Bean                           $12.95

**Intimate Invasions: The Ins and Outs of
Erotic Enema Play**
M.R. Strict                                      $13.95

**The Kinky Girl's Guide to Dating**
Luna Grey                                      $16.95

**The Loving Dominant**
John & Libby Warren                 $16.95

**The Mistress Manual**
Mistress Lorelei                           $16.95

**The New Bottoming Book
The New Topping Book**
Dossie Easton & Janet W.
Hardy                             $14.95 ea.

**Play Piercing**
Deborah Addington                   $13.95

**Radical Ecstasy: SM Journeys to Transcendence**
Dossie Easton & Janet W. Hardy     $16.95

**The Seductive Art of Japanese Bondage**
Midori, photographs by C. Morey     $27.95

**The Sexually Dominant Woman: A Workbook for Nervous Beginners**
Lady Green                                    $11.95

**SM 101: A Realistic Introduction**
Jay Wiseman                               $24.95

**21st Century Kinkycrafts**
edited by Janet Hardy                $19.95

## GENERAL SEXUALITY

**The Ethical Slut: A Guide to Infinite Sexual Possibilities**
Dossie Easton & Catherine A. Liszt   $16.95

**Fantasy Made Flesh: The Essential Guide to Erotic Roleplay**
Deborah Addington                   $13.95

**A Hand in the Bush: The Fine Art of Vaginal Fisting**
Deborah Addington                   $13.95

**Paying For It: A Guide By Sex Workers for Their Customers**
edited by Greta Christina           $13.95

**Phone Sex: Oral Thrills and Aural Skills**
Miranda Austin                           $15.95

**Sex Disasters... And How to Survive Them**
C. Moser, Ph.D., M.D. & J. Hardy   $16.95

**Tricks... To Please a Man
Tricks... To Please a Woman**
both by Jay Wiseman           $13.95 ea.

**When Someone You Love Is Kinky**
Dossie Easton & C. A. Liszt        $15.95

## TOYBAG GUIDES:
**A Workshop In A Book**              **$9.95 each**

**Canes and Caning,** by Janet Hardy

**Clips and Clamps,** by Jack Rinella

**Dungeon Emergencies & Supplies,** by Jay Wiseman

**Erotic Knifeplay,** by Miranda Austin and Sam Atwood

**Foot and Shoe Worship,** by Midori

**High-Tech Toys,** by John Warren

**Hot Wax and Temperature Play,** by Spectrum

**Medical Play,** by Tempest

**Parties and Events,** by Lucullus

## FICTION

**... But I Know What You Want: 25 Sex Tales for the Different**
James Williams                            $13.95

**Love, Sal: letters from a boy in The City**
Sal Iacopelli, ill. Phil Foglio        $13.95

**Murder At Roissy**
John Warren                                  $15.95

**Haughty Spirit
The Warrior Within
The Warrior Enchained**
all by Sharon Green              $11.95 ea.

Please include $3 for first book and $1 for each additional book with your order to cover shipping and handling costs, plus $10 for overseas orders. VISA, MC, AmEx & Discover accepted. Order from Greenery Press, 4200 Park Blvd. pmb 240, Oakland, CA 510/530-1281.